Renters Unite!

T0334777

Renters Unite!

How Tenant Unions are Fighting the Housing Crisis

Jacob Stringer

PLUTO PRESS

First published 2025 by Pluto Press
New Wing, Somerset House, Strand, London WC2R 1LA
and Pluto Press, Inc.
1930 Village Center Circle, 3-834, Las Vegas, NV 89134

www.plutobooks.com

British Library Cataloguing in Publication Data
A catalogue record for this book is available from the British Library

ISBN 978 0 7453 5001 1   Paperback
ISBN 978 0 7453 5003 5   PDF
ISBN 978 0 7453 5002 8   EPUB

This book is printed on paper suitable for recycling and made from fully managed and sustained forest sources. Logging, pulping and manufacturing processes are expected to conform to the environmental standards of the country of origin.

Typeset by Stanford DTP Services, Northampton, England

Simultaneously printed in the United Kingdom and United States of America

Contents

List of Acronyms and Abbreviations

ACORN   Association of Community Organizations for Reform Now

ATUN   Autonomous Tenant Union Network (North America, RSIA in Spanish)

BPW   Bond Precaire Woonvormen (Union of Precarious Tenants, the Netherlands)

CASA   Community Action for Safe Apartments (the Bronx, New York)

CATU   Community Action Tenant Union (Ireland)

CHTU   Crown Heights Tenant Union (New York)

DWE   Deutsche Wohnen & Co. Enteignen (Expropriate Deutsche Wohnen, Berlin)

GLC   Greater London Council

GMTU   Greater Manchester Tenant Union

LATU   Los Angeles Tenant Union

LRU   London Renters Union

MST   Movimento dos Trabalhadores Rurais Sem Terra (Landless Workers Movement, Brazil)

PAH   Plataforma de Afectados por La Hipoteca (Spain)

TANC   Tenant and Neighborhood Committees (Bay Area, California)

Acknowledgements

My heartfelt gratitude goes to everyone in London Renters Union for the years of comradeship and collective action, and for creating an organisation that has absorbed and inspired me for years. I also want to thank those in other tenant unions I spoke to either formally or informally over the years. In the text itself I have largely made the choice not to name the organisers I am quoting or referring to. Some of them have a higher profile than others, both within the organisations and beyond, and most quotes are anonymous so that they can be judged on their own merits. But I want to extend thanks to various interlocuters over the years, who know who they are: Paddy, Bekah, Simon, Michael, Ygerne, Ali, Lucy, Zad, Alva, Amy, Kenny, Jacob, Patch, Meg, Gordon, Joel, Javi, Zara, Isaac, Fiadh, Dont, Tracy, Katrina, Bryan, Abel, Seamus, Ed, Jaime, Peter, Morgan, Irene, Ana, Mara and Adriana.

I also want to particularly thank my partner, Tess, whose understanding and support has enabled me to continue writing, and my daughter, who was too young to know why I sometimes disappeared upstairs to sit at a computer but who might have preferred that I didn't.

I am also grateful to my editor, David Shulman, to Dont Rhine for insightful comments during the drafting, and to the whole team at Pluto for the work they've put into making this book a success.

Preface

It was only once I started organising with a tenant union that I understood the reality of London's housing crisis. Homelessness in the UK often doesn't manifest as street homelessness, it manifests as overcrowding, unsuitable housing, sofa surfing, emergency accommodation and above all 'temporary accommodation', which people can be in for years while they wait for public housing that may never be offered. Organising in a temporary accommodation block (see Chapter 4) with London Renters Union, I met a mother who felt her recent miscarriage had been caused by the absence of a lift (elevator) in the building. Another mother showed me her anti-depressant pills. 'I know I'm not depressed and my doctor knows I'm not depressed,' she said. 'I'm miserable because I've been made to live in six places in five years and I'm just trying to get my 16-year-old daughter through school.' She was beyond caring about the mould in the flat and the plumbing not working and the poor building security, which is why London Renters Union had been invited to organise in the block. She simply wanted to stay put long enough for her daughter to finish school without facing another move.

This is what I explained to an Argentinian housing activist recently when he asked in puzzlement why he could see little evidence of housing crisis in London. In Latin America, housing crisis manifests in the form of informal settlements, land occupations and people living in shacks made of plastic sheeting. In London, and in much of the Global North outside the US, housing crisis becomes channelled, with the help of scarce public services, into private misery. It is only through organising that this misery becomes fully visible. It is when that misery turns to anger that organising becomes viable. The anger and the fight is not a given. Many people in bad housing are resigned to it. Many of them are marginalised people, all of them poor, and they have been pushed around all their lives. Often they have learnt that fighting back is hopeless. That is what makes tenant unions so important. To organise is to replace the despair with anger, and help channel the anger into creating hope.

Most tenant unions also have their fair share of members with more social and cultural capital, people like me, a straight white man with two degrees and an intense dislike of the systems in which I am supposed to be a winner. I joined London Renters Union in its early stages because I was tired of activist groups that existed in limited social strata that never grew or simply carved out a niche for themselves. I wanted to organise with people who I didn't usually see in left activist circles, and I wanted to organise at scale. Having experienced several waves of protest, from the alter-globalisation movement to the UK student protests, through Occupy and the anti-cuts protests, I had felt ephemeral convergences reach their limits. I wanted to see new institutions grow, controlled by their own base, with resources and strategy and training programmes, forms that had faded on the left with the diminishing of the labour movement. While I am happy whenever labour movement activity is resurgent, I saw a need among workforces chopped up by casualisation to organise beyond the workplace. Furthermore, it was clear to me that a vast impoverishment of large numbers of people in 'rich' countries was happening through the medium of rent.

Apparently such thoughts were in the air, for across the Global North tenant unions had begun springing up. For many years, whenever I travelled I checked in on local political activity. As I became more involved in a tenant union myself, this increasingly became about meeting local tenant organisers. I also began to study my own union through academic research. So it was that, without planning it, I drifted into a position where I could write about the rise of a new wave of tenant unions. They were all different and adapted to their local conditions, but had many features in common too. For many of the organisers starting these tenant unions, I discovered, it was not just about facing the seemingly permanent, ever-growing housing crisis, but about rebuilding left-wing movements through organising around everyday needs. The unions were emerging from similar political conditions in their localities, all arising from the complex set of processes that have sometimes been called 'globalisation'.

To start a tenant union is to place a number of bets: that the housing crisis will not solve itself, that ordinary people will fight for what they need, that people still want to build solidarity through larger organisations. These bets have paid off around the world, making tenant unions one of the most exciting social movement developments of recent years. The electoral prospects of the left in countries of the Global North wax and wane – alas mostly the latter recently – but extra-parliamentary organising such as through tenant unions invest in the long term. In these new unions, we see that it is possible to build a political base for a society that rejects the cruelties of neoliberal marketisation. Some housing wins can be quick – stopping a particular eviction or getting a block repaired – but the bigger struggle will last for years, probably decades. Tenant unions make possible both improvements to individuals' lives in the short term and practical hope for the future. I believe every tenant should join a union, not as some act of self-sacrifice but because, as we build solidarity within and between communities, we can all offer each other a chance of a different and better way of organising the world. Renters of the world unite!

1

Why Now?

On a typical suburban street with an atypically spectacular mountain backdrop, a diverse group of people has gathered holding placards and chanting slogans. They are at an apartment complex in Tucson, Arizona, to protest against a management company which has been hiking rents by huge amounts. One former tenant, Cathy, tells a news camera that she got her rent rise the day before Christmas Eve, finding it after returning from a Christmas party. She opened the letter and burst into tears. Now she can't find another place to live and has moved in with her mother. The management company insists that this is just the market, it's just business. They have put her apartment on the market for 50 per cent more than the old rent.[1] But the people out on the street today are tired of being told it's the fault of the market. This is Tucson Tenants Union in action, some members being residents of the apartment block, others here in solidarity. Their demands are modest: to ask for more time for priced-out residents to find new homes. Many are elderly or disabled and their lives are being turned upside down; they have few resources to cushion the shock. In one of the richest countries in the world, vulnerable people are being made homeless every day. According to Diego Martinez-Lugo of Tucson Tenants Union:

> This is why cities, neighborhoods, and communities urgently need tenants unions: to fight capital's incessant displacement, dispossession, and invasion into our homes and communities. Tenants unions, such as the Tucson Tenants Union, are building tenant power not just to resist, but also to collectively imagine and construct a world in which housing is a human right: housing to house and affirm the lives of its inhabitants.[2]

In response to the suffering of those abandoned by the system, a new generation of tenant unions has emerged to take the fight to the landlords. Small as this protest is, it is part of a growing movement: tenants are taking to the streets every day somewhere in the world to assert their right to housing. Tucson Tenants Union is a member of ATUN, the Autonomous Tenant Union Network of North America, a new network of radical tenant unions determined to fight back against housing crisis, personal and general. In turn, the North American tenant unions are just one part of a rising tide of tenant unions around the world.

It is no coincidence that these new tenant unions are springing up at the same time on different continents. From Barcelona to Los Angeles, from Vancouver to Sydney, housing crisis has taken cities of the Global North in its grip. In any city that is desirable as a place to live and work, the rents have been rising, sometimes for decades. The rent rises have followed house price rises, and in their wake have followed the curses of homelessness, overcrowding, slum conditions and abusive landlords. Only in countries without welfare safety nets like the US does this result in a large street-dwelling population. In other rich countries, homelessness is 'neater', it becomes 'hidden homelessness' in which millions of people live in unsuitable accommodation they wouldn't choose to occupy. It looks like two families occupying an apartment designed for one. It looks like teenagers driven out of their homes by violence, sleeping on a sofa at a friend's house. It looks like a four-child family in a two-bedroom house. It looks like a disabled tenant trapped in a second floor home with no lift, unable to move because their income is too low. Under economic systems that thrive on oppressing certain groups, the degradation in housing conditions is experienced unevenly. In the UK, 1.1 million households live in accommodation that is overcrowded by the government's own definition, with those of South Asian and African origin experiencing vastly more overcrowding than those who give their ethnicity as 'White British'.[3]

Even where people are adequately housed for the moment, the threat of victimisation by landlords or of eviction hangs over millions. 'Revenge evictions' from landlords annoyed about requests for repairs or assertions of rights are commonplace. If tenants in London are asked why they don't force the landlord to fix the broken stairs or the leaking taps the answers are always the same: *if they get annoyed at the request they might evict us,* or *if they make the place nicer they'll know they can charge more rent and we'll have to leave.* This housing precarity is very much normalised. One member of my branch of the London Renters Union told me they had always felt this way about asking their landlord for repairs but simply hadn't thought much about it: 'When I joined the union I thought I hadn't had a bad time renting. Then as I got involved I realised that I actually have a bad landlord. I shouldn't be feeling like this.'

Meanwhile, rents have been shooting up in many cities to astonishingly high levels. In London in 2022, the average cost for a one-bedroom flat was 44 per cent of the median pay – and that's the percentage of pay before tax. By 2024, as I write this book, the situation is worse, and it isn't uncommon for rent to take up well over half of a tenant's income. At this level of rent, quality of life inevitably declines. Tenants living with high rents not only can't afford a decent standard of living in the present, they are also prevented from advancing themselves in the future, since they can never grow their savings. Having to pay rent is like living with a crushing debt that can never be fully repaid. In the UK, there is still low-cost council housing remaining, but an ever-diminishing number as estates get 'regenerated' and homes sold off. Now council tenants who can't possibly afford private sector rents get forced out of London, or risk losing their place on the housing list. London is not for them, they are told, always implicitly, sometimes explicitly. They are left high and dry in cities where they know no one, their children forced to start school again in a new place. Community is eroded and life becomes mere survival. This is no way for millions of people to live in supposedly rich countries. But it just keeps getting worse.

In Barcelona, a family is evicted to make way for short-term holiday letting. They'll struggle to get another home because a lot of places they might have moved to have also become holiday lets. In Brooklyn, the residents of a rent-controlled block find themselves unable to get repairs from their landlord or agent, who consider that they should just be grateful for their below-market rent. Any resident who calls asking for repairs is treated with contempt. In Glasgow, a tenant finds that the estate agent has arranged viewings of their flat without even telling them they are being evicted. The rent is going up and the agent knew they couldn't pay. Like many renters across the world, the tenants suddenly understand that it was a mistake to view this flat as their home. In Vancouver, it only dawns on residents that they are about to be evicted when they see a notice of redevelopment posted on the door. In some sense, they had been expecting it for years, their low-rise block now out of place among new high-rises, yet in a way it would have been better if the notice had come earlier. Now there is nowhere within a half hour ride that they can afford. In Berlin, a tenant discovers they are illegally sub-letting their room from someone who has it at a controlled rent. They decide that they won't report their landlord's failure to check the gas boiler, unsure of their rights. In Dublin, a mother peruses the property listings for a place that can accommodate her second child on her budget, and realises she will have to stay in her one-bedroom home. She prays that she won't be evicted because her next home will be even smaller than this.

What links all these places, besides the miserable and insecure living conditions of a large section of the population? They have all been afflicted by what some scholars call 'hyper-gentrification', one feature of which is that gentrification and huge property price rises are not limited to one section of a city but spread across the whole of it like a plague, with even middle-class people forced out by higher earners. To describe that process more bluntly, money has poured into property across cities and continents like a never-ending waterfall, like a veritable Niagara Falls. Housing has come to be seen as a global 'asset class', a repository for the money of investors not just locally but across the world. This is a result not only of vast amounts of wealth swilling around the global economy, but of an establishment politics, almost ubiquitous in rich countries, of believing that the market was best placed to provide and set the price of housing. If this process sounds like it does not discriminate, the opposite is in fact true, for the effects of housing crisis are always unevenly distributed along lines of class and race and gender wherever they arise. Those most affected are those whose lives are already hard. The accumulation of wealth by landlords comes at the cost of dispossession.

I asked one mother waiting for a council house in temporary accommodation in London what she thought housing should look like. She was living in a poorly maintained old block that had been left to rot. The roof leaked, the lifts broke down all the time, and drug users, similarly abandoned by the state, barged their way through security doors and used the corridors and stairwells to get high. Her answer was simple and straightforward:

You know, clean housing, homely housing, houses that people could be happy to come back to, so at work you're looking forward to coming home because it's a good home, housing where children can have a bit of place to actually play.

This heartbreaking and modest demand for what housing should be was spoken as though it were an almost utopian dream, a longing for something she knew was out of her reach. In one of the richest countries on earth, ordinary people with jobs and families dream of a simple but better life, and it is constantly out of reach.

LOCAL TO GLOBAL CRISES

Lack of housing or inadequate housing blights lives. Being unhoused outdoors means facing endless dangers, ranging from anti-poor assault, through police violence, to hypothermia and other potentially life-threatening health problems. But even inadequate housing can present many dangers. This brings us to another more hidden element of housing crisis – hidden, at least, to those who make no effort to investigate, which includes most politicians and media voices. Much housing for those on low income is very poorly maintained. In the UK, this 'disrepair crisis' all too often applies to social housing as much as the private rented sector. Private landlords are failing to do basic maintenance to keep properties safe, and not only do municipal authorities fail in their role as regulator of the private rented sector, but those same authorities are not even maintaining their own properties. To some extent, both failures can be laid at the feet of the 'austerity' programmes imposed by central government, but also to poor prioritisation. Disrepair is robbing people of their security at home, but it is happening to people who just don't matter very much.

Health problems from damp and mould are rife – 900,000 households in England suffer from serious damp and mould[4] – and they can prove deadly. In the UK, the case of Awaab Ishak was widely reported in an unusual case of housing disrepair hitting the headlines. Awaab lived in a one-bedroom flat with his parents, their landlord a Rochdale housing association – a type of non-profit social housing provider that has become increasingly financialised in recent years. When Awaab's father complained to the housing association about the damp, he was told to paint over the mould. Awaab died, aged two, from a severe respiratory condition brought on by black mould in his home. The case is justly famous, partly because the courts on this occasion pinned the blame squarely on the landlord. Many children had died previously of mould without the courts satisfactorily addressing the issue. The case received enough attention that the government passed a law requiring social landlords to remedy damp and mould within particular timeframes. But this is plugging just one hole in a system in which tenants are routinely ignored when they ask for maintenance of their homes, including the basic repairs necessary to bring their property up to a liveable standard.

Even more famously, the appalling Grenfell Tower tragedy took the highest toll of any housing disaster in UK history and the images of it flashed around the world. Seventy-two tenants died, many of them in a state of terror and agony that scarcely bears thinking about. The failure to properly care for tenants could no longer ignored, but it was too late for Grenfell. A culture of seeing tenants who asked for improvements as troublesome had embedded itself within the social landlord organisation, Kensington and Chelsea Tenant Management Organisation (TMO), and this converged with the erosion of building standards in the UK to cause a calamity that echoes down through the years, too painful to ever be forgotten.

The fire at Grenfell Tower was the worst residential fire in the UK since the Second World War, but the events that led up to it are far from unique: neglect of tenants is everyday, endemic and unceasing. Respiratory health and fire present only the most obvious menaces to forgotten tenants. Other dangers, arising from cold, heat and hygiene issues, are equally common, and wear away at health and well-being. Many tenants live with very high levels of stress due to poor maintenance, abusive landlords and chronically insecure living conditions. Discrimination by race, or by class, against people with disabilities or against those on welfare is rife. Tenants have told me that their lives feel on hold. They don't feel they can live fully until they get safe, secure, adequate accommodation. Why has it been denied to them in wealthy countries that could afford to house them, and why has it happened so consistently across so much of the Global North?

I have carefully described gentrification as an influx of money because commentators are often distracted by the surface manifestations of gentrification: fancy coffee shops and bars, or the pricing out of local businesses in favour of chains and upmarket food outlets. Changes in a community are sometimes blamed on the new business owners, or on local planning policy, or on the new block of flats that was built down the road, or on the selling of some public housing. While it can be useful for campaigning purposes to find local antagonists, it is also worth zooming out and looking at the bigger picture. What we have been witnessing is a seismic political and economic shift in cities across the globe. We are in the age of the rentier, and whatever proximal causes we find locally it also can't be a coincidence that this is now true across most of the Global North. Something bigger has been at work.

The stance that mainstream economists and politicians take on these unfolding crises of unaffordable and inadequate housing is that there simply aren't enough houses. In their view, the solution to high house prices is always that more housing needs to be built. The laws of supply and demand are, after all, immutable. To many people, this feels intuitively correct and journalists on daily news programmes are apt to parrot it as though fact. But if one thinks about this for more than a moment, a niggling doubt creeps in. Surely some country, somewhere in the world, must have built its way out of housing crisis by now. In all the wide world, surely some government took the bull by the horns and ensured a supply of the housing people needed, and now everyone there is living in good-quality, affordable housing. If the economists are correct, some country must at least have allowed the developers to build as much as demand dictated. Well, yes and no.

Alas, no, there is no country that has built its way out of the housing crisis. There is a country – Spain – where the developers were allowed to build as much as they wanted. Furthermore, the deregulated banks began giving mortgages to higher and higher risk buyers, just as they had in the US to precipitate the wider global crisis. This over-development plus lax mortgage regulation led in 2011 to ... housing crisis, in the form of evictions, repossessions and crashing prices leaving people in negative equity. The case of Spain reminds us that the price of housing is to a large extent set by the willingness of mortgage lenders to lend. Did the low prices after the crash at least give more people access to housing? Also no. In fact, in 2017, the United Nations (UN) declared Spain in violation of its duty to provide the right to adequate housing when a family with a young child were evicted from private rented accommodation in Madrid, having been waiting in vain for one of the few publicly owned homes to become available, unable to afford to buy themselves.

The problem was that 'la crisis' in Spain didn't only affect housing. It also created massive unemployment, and unemployed people can't get mortgages even for low-priced housing. It also turned out that much of the newer housing was built in the wrong places, and where banks had repossessed properties in large numbers, they had clung onto the empty housing in the hope of future price rises. As a result, many parts of Spain – the parts with more jobs – still had a housing scarcity problem. The reckless unleashing of the market had led to catastrophe rather than solving the housing problems.

This is not to say that there is never an undersupply of housing and that more housing doesn't need to be built in many cities. Often housing campaigners want to focus on getting people into existing empty homes, or ending short-term lets or second home ownership. These are important, both in housing and political terms, but even if all these things were done in a city such as London, there would still be a scarcity of housing. New renters keep entering the market as they move to London or leave parental homes, and those who used to buy their way out of renting into home ownership are trapped there, so the number of renters keeps on increasing.

Migration too can be a part of the picture, and we needn't react to that by railing against migrants. Rather, if governments know there is net immigration, they should be building the housing (and public services) to match. Given that they are expanding their tax base with immigration this shouldn't be too much to ask. Unfortunately, the right-wing narratives around immigration often obscure this common sense solution, and the left often responds simply by saying that 'immigrants aren't the problem'. This is true, but if the population of a city is expanding, whether due to migration or birth rate, then the expansion of the city needs to be planned. We know by now that the market doesn't make the necessary adjustments to housing stock, whatever fantasies students are taught in Economics 101 classes.

Left-wing campaigners are also keen not to end up on the same side as the YIMBY (Yes In My Backyard) pro-developer lobby. But it is easy to differentiate left-wing campaigning from YIMBY campaigning: it simply demands good-quality public or collectively owned housing rather than more market housing that will be snapped up by speculators. A big problem with new-build market housing in many countries right now is that landlords often have more capital than ordinary people, and frequently outbid them, but that doesn't mean more housing shouldn't be built in cities with growing populations. It should just be the housing that is actually needed. Capitalism has a tendency to create scarcity where there could be abundance, and this is the case in housing as with other goods. Sometimes housing scarcity is an illusion brought on by the madness of the markets, but sometimes the scarcity is real and means the rich always outcompete the poor for property. This shouldn't distract us from talking about the distribution of housing ownership and the destructiveness of the current distribution.

One tenant, a Black woman and a mother, who I spoke to in London, whose home was constantly in disrepair, had a good instinct for the deeper causes of her situation. 'I see inequality is part of the problem … campaigning around inequality is very important.' Poor housing options are not just a result of inequality though, they are also a cause of inequality. 'You work but you're not seeing the money, the priority is paying rent,' she said with an angry shake of her head. This describes the downward spiral many tenants find themselves in. They can't better their housing situation because all their money is disappearing in rent for their current housing. If the economy is in a phase of rising salaries, rents will inevitably be rising too, so the only beneficiaries of those rises are landlords. The despair of that tenant was palpable, knowing as she did that no matter how hard she works, her children will not benefit, only her landlord.

One theme I will develop in this book is that it is important to develop a wide lens on the multiple housing crises we face. Many British housing campaigners, if asked why this tenant can't have good housing, will answer that it is because Margaret Thatcher and her successors sold off council housing while preventing the building of new public housing. This is in some sense true, for the tenant is on the waiting list for council housing and if there were more available she would not have to live for so many years in precarious housing with disrepair that often drives her to despair. But when I asked residents in Buenos Aires why housing in the centre of the city was almost as expensive as London, forcing people out to the suburbs, they told me it was because rich soya-growers were buying up all the property, while in Barcelona they explained it as the rise of Airbnb. These reasons are also true, but surely do not reach far enough in explaining the overall global trends. There must be bigger economic patterns, not to say failures, at play for decent homes to become so inaccessible across so much of the 'rich' world.

As an important aside, I want to point out that most of the large-scale housing organising in the world right now takes place in the Global South. Brazil, India, South Africa and a host of other countries have movements achieving enormous amounts in housing, and often linked to wider movements that are challenging power in inspiring ways. I will not discuss these movements much in this book, mostly because lack of space compels me to narrow my focus. It is also the case that the particular conditions under which people fight make a difference to what they are able to do. Much organising in the Global South takes place where the state is indifferent or incompetent or in flux. This creates very different opportunities for action than for those under long-entrenched state institutions in the Global North who are highly capable of getting what they want – alas, usually not good housing. In addition, organising in the Global South often relies on the fact that societies have not yet been so shattered by consumerist individualism as societies in the Global North. Communities often organise because they are already communities, and because people live communally to some degree already. Nonetheless, the range of organising across the Global South presents a huge array of ways people have taken action and thought about their housing problems – far too great a range for me to discuss here. I encourage anyone interested in reading about housing movements of the Global South to start with the readable *Urban Warfare* by Raquel Rolnik[5] and to move on to the many excellent case studies of housing and land movements across the world, from Brazil's MST to South Africa's Abahlali base Mjondolo.

LOCAL TO GLOBAL CAUSES

Margeret Thatcher's fire sale of council housing in the UK was certainly mirrored in some other countries by the sell-off and neglect of existing public housing, and above all a failure to build more. But neoliberalism is enacted differently in different places, and takes on a local character. In some countries, like Spain, public housing had rarely been an important part of the tenure mix, while in others, like France, public housing is still operating at scale. Yet an apartment in Paris can cost just as much as in London, where much council housing has been sold into private hands. So what else is going on? The deeper problems arose because the erosion of public housing unfailingly came along with the whole package of the Thatcherite–Reaganite neoliberal revolution. At the same time that Thatcher was selling off council housing and killing rent controls, she and her compatriots around the world were initiating processes more powerful even than those policies. They were kicking off a new wave of a particular type of globalisation: unfettered global trade and finance. The full consequences of that are only just being realised.

Take the Heygate Estate in London, a huge 1960s council estate just outside central London in the Elephant and Castle area, with 1200 flats built around leafy green courtyards. Its destruction and replacement with luxury flats and high-end food outlets can be read as a local story. In the local story, the estate had been denigrated as a problematic 'sink estate' for years, though not everyone agreed, and one study suggested its crime rate was half that of the borough of Southwark in which it sits. The real problem, campaigners said, was lack of care from the council, who had chosen managed decline for the estate. Southwark council seemed to be somewhere between highly incompetent and corrupt, with 'gifts' going to the council leader and senior officers moving between 'public service' and lucrative jobs for developers. The land was sold off far too cheaply on the promise of plenty of affordable homes. The fightback from tenants was extensive and highly publicised, even bold and inspiring, with some holdouts finally squatting in some of the empty properties to delay their destruction – I visited while activists were practising tree-climbing in order to occupy the trees of the 'Heygate Forest' to delay the bulldozers – but the local council wasn't listening.

Now the Heygate Estate is gone and has been replaced with the privatised 'Elephant Park', marketed to workers in the City of London. Former tenants have been scattered to the four winds, almost all of them pushed further out from the centre of London. This has been documented extensively by local campaign groups such as the 35% Campaign that tries to force the developer to make good on its promises of 35 per cent affordable housing. But many of the promised affordable housing options have failed to materialise, or been undermined, and the local council seems unable or unwilling to enforce their own planning rules.

But there is another way to tell the story of the Heygate Estate, as a more global story. In this story, the Heygate Estate is an area of housing for poor people set within walking distance, or two or three tube stops, of one of the richest financial centres on the planet. It had a sword of Damocles hanging over it. In the financial centre of the City of London, hundreds of thousands of workers earned well above average wages. Their wealth spilt out around and beyond London, with everywhere within commutable distance seeing rocketing house prices to match their rocketing incomes. The local authority, meanwhile, had been starved of funds by central government and lack of tax-raising powers. In an age of abundance, it had been forced into a situation of scarcity, and of enforcing scarcity on others. The Elephant and Castle area was convenient not only for the workers but for companies who wanted to buy places for corporate guests to stay in. The Heygate site, expensive to maintain in its current form, was a sure-fire money-maker as a development site.

Granted confidence by that knowledge of a wealthy salaried class and wealthy corporations, it wasn't long before the developers came sniffing. It was Lendlease, a company headquartered in Australia, who won the bidding, and one can imagine executives in plush offices looking at the location of the estate on a map and rubbing their hands in glee. They made themselves very friendly with the local council, getting a price for the land that made their profits certain. They had no trouble obtaining finance in the City, which had a surplus of capital to dispose of; as the construction went ahead, they were already selling the luxury flats. Many of them were sold 'off-plan', without even being seen, mostly to overseas investors in China or Singapore. Like many developers now, Lendlease uses globalised estate agents, such as Knight Frank, with offices around the world so that they can sell their properties in as many markets as possible.

Old money and new from all over the world poured into Elephant Park, buying one-bedroom flats for half a million pounds, penthouses for over a million. Most of those investors will rent out the flats to those working in well-paid industries such as finance and tech. The landlords will make money. Lendlease makes money. Their shareholders make money. Knight Frank makes money. Torrents of money flow all around the world, all activated by the cannibalisation of 'redevelopment', the waste and destruction all necessary to get a return on capital. From one perspective, the Heygate Estate/Elephant Park becomes a mere funnel for quantities of finance beyond the comprehension of those who once lived there. The local authority, meanwhile, continues to be starved of funds, even as a new generation of local politicians attempts to build a little more housing to make up for the sins of their forebears. A new world is being shaped, and ensuring the right to housing for ordinary people is not a part of it.

What neoliberal globalisation achieved, in some countries backed by a claimed need for 'austerity', was to globalise inequality as it globalised trade and finance. Austerity, of course, was just the ideology of small government (for the poor) in new clothing. Neoliberalism, as opposed to capitalism in general, is defined by a fixation on small government and minimal regulation, while not actually shrinking government but shifting public resources to support corporate power through forced marketisation, open borders for capital but not people, and outsourcing. Neoliberalism as a reaction against social democracy created, quite deliberately, a world of winners and losers and ensured that the winners would have global reach while the losers would have the little they had taken from them. It was clear enough that this was happening 25 years ago. An entire movement, the alter-globalisation movement of the 1990s and early 2000s, rose up against it. But the ideologues in government believed they knew best, that in the end the market would make everyone richer. In reality, it made some people richer, and it made a few people very rich indeed. The rest were left behind.

So it is that on a walk along Venice Boardwalk, a beach-front tourist attraction in Los Angeles, I walk past encampments where people live in tents designed to be used for a few nights a year. The camps are interwoven with upmarket bars and cafes. Along Mulholland Drive and Laurel Canyon in the mountains above, sprawling mansions with infinity pools look out towards Venice Beach. This is one of the richest cities in the world. The tents are invisible at such a distance, but the rich know they are there. Even in the US, which likes to ignore its poor, the encampments found throughout Los Angeles can't be ignored. They are a topic of political discussion in part because they 'ruin' downtown LA or attractive places like Venice Beach. The most common political response is more policing. The rich decide that the police should steal the few belongings that the poor have, in order to make them go away. Where to? Few people care. This is inequality writ large: people who inhabit entirely different universes, yet pass each other in the street. Some of the rich who make the decisions to steal from the poor might even work in the same building as a worker living in their car. They do not talk to each other because inequality begets social stratification, not to say isolation. Their worlds drift further apart, along with any hope of a coherent democratic encounter between them.

In London, a woman named Katy (name changed) in receipt of housing benefit wanted to rent a flat. The letting agent for the flat, like most letting agents, didn't like the fact that Katy was in receipt of welfare, so they asked for six months' rent in advance. This is a widespread practice, despite being discriminatory against people on welfare, and Katy realised that she wouldn't be able to rent a flat without doing it, so she borrowed thousands of pounds from friends and family in order to secure herself a home. But what the letting agent was doing that was different to other agents, and which was hidden away in the small print of Katy's contract, was that they were going to continue to charge her six months' rent in advance every six months. Katy had handed over money to secure the flat before seeing the contract; when she did see it, she was very hesitant to sign. Over the course of a four-hour meeting the estate agent bullied her into signing the contract. At one point, according to a friend who was with her, an agent said, 'I'm going on a holiday, I've got a plane to catch. You've got 15 minutes to sign this tenancy agreement.'

Under this pressure Katy signed, but when she had time to think about it, she knew that paying six months' rent upfront every six months was simply unattainable for her, as it would be for most people. Katy felt she had no option but to pull out of the contract without moving into the flat. But because she had signed the contract, the letting agent decided to keep over £6000 of her money, much of which she had borrowed. The flat was let to someone else anyway, so the landlord was not out of pocket. But Katy's life was devastated by the decision to keep her money. She went to the local community advice centres but they all said the same thing: you signed the contract, legally they are in the right, there's nothing we can do. Whether the contract signed was truly fair, and under fair conditions, was debatable, but Katy couldn't afford to go to court to fight that battle – it would have cost more than the money she had already lost. Someone with much more money and power than Katy had decided that they would ruin her financially because they could. They seemed to care not at all for Katy's plight. She was, it seemed, beneath them. A mere low-income tenant.

But the story didn't end there. Katy joined London Renters Union and the union fought tooth and nail to get her money back. It was of no interest to the union that the letting agent might be legally within their rights. The union understood this as what it was: a matter of power. A question of asserting that Katy's life mattered. It took months to get that money back. It took protests at the letting agent, shutting them down for the day, it took a telephone blockade of the offices, it took a Google review blitz. The union made it clear that it would not give up, that the power of the union was on Katy's side, and so it was that the letting agent folded and gave her back every penny of her money. But just imagine the kind of parasitic mindset those letting agents had to be in to get to such a situation: they had to see Katy as nobody, as barely human, as just another mark. This is where the gross inequality of tenant and landlord leads: a basic failure of decency, an inability by those at the top to understand that those beneath them are human.

THE RENTIER ECONOMY

The generalised inequality offered by neoliberalism, made vivid in workplaces like Amazon warehouses where people are treated as human robots, is considerably worsened by property-driven inequality. The enclosure and accumulation of property creates a multiplier effect for all existing inequality. David Harvey refers to cities as acting as 'sponges' for capital,[6] particularly when there is a lack of other investment opportunities. As the rich get richer, they need places to put their money. Some of it does go into industry, but there were never going to be enough business opportunities to soak up all the money being hoarded. Besides, businesses can fail, while property just stays right there (or at least the land does, which is often the most valuable bit), so for investors, both expert and inexpert, property increasingly came to be seen as a safe bet.

As if that wasn't enough money flowing into property, the deregulation of financial services enabled banks to come up with ever-more ways to lend money against property, bringing new money into existence solely for the purpose of inflating property markets. Huge investment funds such as Blackstone and Black-Rock began to target residential as well as commercial property. Real Estate Investment Trusts (REITs) grew and grew. Developers and financiers began to see the appeal of build-to-rent apartment blocks, establishing returns on capital that would flow in perpetuity. Public housing was sold to profit-making companies, and financialisation was even able to creep into the non-profit sector like the UK's housing associations, which were forced to act like profit-making companies due to having to borrow money on the markets rather than from government. The degree of financialisation of housing became so intense that former UN Rapporteur Raquel Rolnik titled her book: *Urban Warfare: Housing under the Empire of Finance*. The empire reaches every inhabited continent on earth.

Most of the cost of any house in a desirable place to live will be the cost of the land rather than the cost of construction. Land goes up in value as society gets richer because it is both scarce (in places where people want to live) and necessary. As wealth goes up, the claims upon land become greater, and we shouldn't be surprised by that under a market system. To some extent, land prices have gone up for the same reason that the price of single malt whisky has been going up for a couple of decades: the world produces more and more consumers rich enough to buy it. But this is looking at demand at an aggregate level, when a key part of the story of what has happened to land and property is its *distribution*. Land is not a luxury good but a necessity, yet it is increasingly hoarded by a certain segment of society. And there is a key difference between land and other goods: unlike other commodities it is not destroyed in the use of it. So the scarcity of land, the permanence of it and the necessity of it for living open up the possibility for something not all commodities can yield: rent.

Put differently, there are two markets for housing: one, a market for people buying places they need to live in, the other a market for investors and speculators seeking rent. The supply and demand in these two markets affect each other, but it is important to distinguish them because once we do so, certain features of the 'housing market' become clearer. The demand from investors and speculators is often greater than the demand for housing, by which I mean that they have more money to offer. So the demand from landlords pushes up prices so that however much people 'demand' a house to live in, the price they can pay will never be enough. This is true even if many more houses are built. Land and property that people need can *de facto* be held hostage by the class of people that can afford to own it, forcing those who can't to pay well over the odds for a roof over their head. Thus, we arrive at the age of the rentier, an age in which it is easier to make money from rent than from productive investment. The age of the rentier, to be clear, is not just about property. Much of what happens in the economy and financial markets is various forms of rent-seeking. All that money at the top of society not only flows into land and property, but into other assets too, such as privatised formerly public services, and enables those with big money to monopolise the necessities of life.

While for most people the rise of unearned income over earned income – and the dehumanisation that goes along with the subsequent inequality – instinctively seems like a bad idea, the market fundamentalists have now been in charge for so long that the gross distortions of the economy from rent are dismissed with glib remarks about how the 'invisible hand' of the market knows what it is doing. For those with deeper knowledge of economics this is risible: every major economist from Adam Smith to John Maynard Keynes has been at pains to point out that no market can really function where the rentier dominates, since their unproductive rent-seeking will distort any attempt to be genuinely productive. The damage this can do was finally nailed down by Thomas Piketty in his magnum opus *Capital in the Twenty-first Century*. In fact, he depicted rent-seeking as the fatal flaw in capitalism if left unchecked, with return on capital eventually coming to dominate, rising higher than economic growth:

[This] implies that wealth accumulated in the past grows more rapidly than output and wages. This inequality expresses a fundamental logical contradiction. The entrepreneur inevitably tends to become a rentier, more and more dominant over those who own nothing but their labour. Once constituted, capital reproduces itself faster than output increases. The past devours the future.[7]

Piketty also draws out the consequences of the rule of the rentier: inequality increases at ever-increasing speed in a doom spiral whereby rentiers can extract ever more from their victims. He is clear too that democracy simply cannot stand up to such astonishing levels of inequality. The huge flow of capital to rentiers will corrupt everything they touch. The economic crisis leads inevitably to a political crisis: the draining of power from everyone but the rentier class.

In some ways, even capitalism isn't really getting what it wants: the rise of the rentier has seen productivity rates drop, increasingly childless cities, with schools shutting across areas that no ordinary person can afford to live in, shrinking populations as people have fewer children and, most damaging of all for capitalist ideology any pretence at meritocracy has been swept away. The children of those with money can buy a home while others struggle along in rented accommodation. A survey published by the *Financial Times* found that while in the 1980s around 20 per cent of people in the UK depended on family to buy their first home, in the 2020s this has shot up to 50 per cent.[8] Many are left unable to buy, putting increased pressure on rental accommodation and increasing rents further. No one can pretend any more that working hard and living a quiet and law-abiding life within the system will enable us to have a good quality of life. However much we earn it will all be sucked up in rent.

In fact, much more of our income will be sucked up in rent than most of us ever realise, for every time we buy a coffee at a coffee shop we are paying rent, every time we buy a pint of beer we are paying rent, and when we decide to shop at Amazon we are, even if we aren't consciously aware of it, making a desperate bid to avoid paying the rent on a high street shop. Piketty's own solutions to this dominance of the rentier are dramatic, if not particularly radical: he proposes a global wealth tax, with land and property being included in the assets to be taxed. Such a tax might save capitalism from itself as Piketty intends, and it might take some pressure off land prices, but it would not ensure access to decent housing for all. Something more is required: a genuine determination to provide housing to all who need it, and the political base to make it happen.

But across much of the world every solution to housing crisis has been politically blocked for a generation. Rent control is not a full solution, but it does make people's lives better. Economists claim it 'doesn't work', staring studiously at their graphs while ignoring all the places in the world where it does work. Real estate developers will stop building houses, they claim, ignoring all the houses built in rent-controlled cities – studies show that new building peaked in New York during years of high rent control. Rent control isn't just about controlling price but also about increasing security by preventing huge leaps in rent. A high rent rise is an eviction for most people.

I recall a new London Renters Union member who had just received a £500 per month rent rise from his landlord. He and his whole family would have to move out from their home 20 minutes from central London to an outer suburb over an hour's travel from his workplace and his friends. He was angry and ready to protest at this drop in his quality of life, ready to shout from a microphone at the injustice of it. But most people go quietly, if cursing 'the market' under their breath. The UK government has promised to end 'no-fault' evictions, in which the landlord doesn't have to give a reason for ending a tenancy, but they perpetually delay it on behalf of landlords. Anyway, if the rent can be raised 30 per cent then they won't have ended arbitrary eviction. Rent control is not just about price *per se*, but about allowing people to stay where they are, about allowing community to develop and survive.

Other solutions are also blocked. Controlling short-term lets so that housing isn't lost should be eminently possible but even in Barcelona, this has been an epic battle and final victory is still elusive. Too many interested parties are lobbying to allow the market – meaning those with the most money – to decide what housing should be used for. In Edinburgh, Living Rent fights a constant battle to get short-term lets like Airbnb regulated. Having won a victory at national level in Scotland, in the form of a framework for regulation, they now have to get local authorities to implement it. The resistance from landlords, some of whom are the politicians making the decisions, must be countered every step of the way. Under pressure from tenant movements, the Scottish government conceded some temporary rent control measures, but the landlords are determined they will be only temporary. Building more publicly owned homes might work in some sense, mainstream economists admit, but it is a 'distortion of the market' or, as ideologies of austerity have become mainstreamed in much of Europe, they have increasingly insisted that 'we can't afford it'. The war in Ukraine or a banking crisis might merit producing billions in extra funding, but a mere housing crisis does not. Every proposal that might really make a difference is dismissed by neoliberal governments as 'not possible' or 'not desirable'.

Housing crisis continues, however, not because governments simply refuse to act, but because they do act. Despite their proclaimed faith in markets, governments actively make housing crisis worse with subsidies such as the UK's 'Help to Buy', a deposit assistance scheme for first-time buyers, which studies show simply increased the price of housing. Meanwhile, tax incentives reward unearned income over earned. Government funds that once went to building public housing get redirected to subsidise landlords. 'Affordable housing' becomes a gamed category knowingly allowed to fatten developers' profits. Should we even call this 'housing crisis' as though it arose by accident and is too hard to solve? Governments are not only ignoring solutions but actively militating to worsen the crisis. Isn't this not so much 'housing crisis' as simply 'housing policy'? Shouldn't we, rather than saying to each other 'the housing crisis is bad', simply be saying to each other 'the housing policy is bad' or 'the housing system is bad'? Arguably, the very framing of 'the housing crisis' is a construct that benefits those in power, since it evades the question of who is responsible and who benefits. 'Housing crisis' is such a commonly used phrase that I will continue to use it, but I use the term here with a particular meaning, and without the indefinite article. 'The housing crisis' is something the establishment can pretend we wandered into by accident. As I use it, 'housing crisis' is the housing injustice that those in power have forced us to live with because it benefits them. It is not a singular crisis but multiple crises, but what unites housing crisis across the globe is that the system is working as intended. It is a bogus crisis for those with power, which is why it is never resolved, but it is a real crisis for us, a state of social conflict that can only be resolved from below.

LOCKED INTO LANDLORDISM

How did countries of the Global North get into such a political mess over a necessity of life, where the eminently resolvable seems so irresolvable? The dream of a 'property-owning democracy', in which one's stake in society is made real in the form of one's own personal piece of real estate, had been held out through much of the twentieth century as an individualist bulwark against too much state intervention. Rather than supposedly domineering welfare states running people's lives, they would have their own asset in the form of a house, a guarantor of independence, both economic and political. This conservative vision, embraced by anti-state free market 'liberals', was given a new lease of life in the 1980s by ideologues such as Thatcher and Reagan and their neoliberal revolution that swept the world. In some sense, the neoliberal evangelists may have believed what they preached: that the only guarantor of freedom was private property, and that everyone should have a chance at owning some. Perhaps they were well intentioned, we might think, though the present housing crises show them to be clearly mistaken.

Yet they weren't *very well* intentioned: if we examine Hayek and Mises and the other philosophers of this new revolution, a common theme emerges. They always understood that there would be winners and losers. They were believers in the spoils going to the strong, and if the weak, like Katy, were swept aside, so be it, that would only make society as a whole stronger. While Hayek deplored state-led eugenics as a tool of totalitarianism, he believed strongly in a kind of eugenics of the market, albeit focused on behaviour rather than genes. The market should be allowed to shape humanity by abandoning those who lacked the behaviours needed to survive, eliminating the weak. This unpleasant philosophy even gained popular cultural traction in the form of Ayn Rand's novels, with *Atlas Shrugged* offering nothing but a big shrug for the suffering of the 'weak' in what she believed to be a civilisation declining due to lack of entrepreneurial drive. Yet this element of Hayek and Mises' philosophy is very much obscured in mainstream teachings of their economics. The focus is always on what the winners deserve, but, of course, that always implies that the losers also get what they deserve, even up to homelessness and starvation. And if that means disproportionately more Black people, or Indigenous people, or single mothers are homeless and starving, well, the neoliberal ideologues were always very relaxed about that.

But while clearly supremacist philosophies underpin the neoliberal revolution, it is not philosophies that prevent housing problems from being solved, it is power relations. The pursuit of 'property-owning democracy' succeeded in many rich countries in creating a homeowner voting bloc that has become unassailable. In the UK in particular, this was very deliberately constructed. Thatcher believed that for every new homeowner she would be creating a new Conservative voter, and the voting tendencies of the following decades would prove her not far wrong. Those who bought the council homes she sold off were indeed grateful for their windfall – a windfall heavily subsidised by the state.

The history of neoliberalism is littered with such ironies. Indeed, it is characteristic of the 'neo' in neoliberalism that the state has often been repurposed as an incentive-provider or a bludgeon to create the 'free' markets that the market fundamentalists believe necessary. This was not entirely new: the homeowner paradises of American suburbs could hardly exist without government subsidies to fossil fuel transport. But this intervention supposedly on behalf of the market is now rampant. Having helped create the supposedly autonomous housing market, the managers of the state then decide that they should step back from it, with the exception, that is, of further public subsidies to privatise publicly owned properties, lax tax regimes, low interest rates, mortgage support, schemes to support new buyers, political support to developers and so on. The reality is that the housing market is and must be constantly created, supported and recreated by state intervention. The 'free' market is an illusion, yet it is an illusion to which most major parties in most rich countries in the world have committed themselves and, *because it benefits particular people or groups, the* illusion must be maintained, and so action on housing becomes heavily circumscribed.

An example of how policy choices become circumscribed at the institutional level comes from the southwest England City of Bristol in 2022. The city council had noted the dire state of the rental market in the city and had set up a Living Rent Commission to try to find solutions. That sounds like a positive step, but the problem was that plenty of landlords had been invited to sit on the commission, while the biggest tenant representative group in Bristol, the community union ACORN, had not been invited at all. This was a recipe, ACORN considered, for yet more 'market-based' solutions and little real change. They voiced their objection to the mayor but were ignored. Next, they turned up at the town hall and protested noisily. Still, the mayor refused to talk to them, though they had simply wanted to put forward to Bristol council the policy demands of the Renter's Reform Coalition, a nationwide network of housing organisations to which they belong.

Some weeks later, ACORN went to the town hall for a big action, shutting down the first meeting of the commission at the town hall and staging a 'Real Renting Commission' meeting, where tenants' voices could truly be heard. Renters stood up and told their stories, often visibly upset by their experiences of the rental market. One woman with fibromyalgia, Jean, spoke of how she had constantly been discriminated against. 'I was literally told by four landlords they would not accept me because I was in receipt of disability benefit. I was very lucky I was able to sofa surf.'[9] This town hall takeover was an inspiring display of defiance by ACORN, but once again the landlords got a seat at the official table while the symbolic broadcasting of the needs of tenants was all that could be achieved. The system consistently denies tenants a voice precisely because the voice of landlords is so loud.

Homeowners, meanwhile, have much more of a voice than tenants, although they are not the biggest beneficiaries of inflationary housing policies. In many countries, the homeowner bloc, which also happens to include the older people who vote more, is a key voter bloc in any election. Any politician who crosses them, as Liz Truss accidentally did in the UK, can expect a very short career in politics. Indeed, in the UK, the common sense of centrist politicians for the last 20 years has been that if they can keep house prices going up, they can hold onto power. The previous big electoral turnaround, from Labour to Conservative, happened in the wake of the financial crisis that caused the only dip in house prices of the last 20 years. The financial crisis was global, and blame could only really be attributed to Labour in the sense that it had gone along with the same neoliberal paradigm that other countries had also been committed to, and to which the Conservatives were even more committed. But I believe it is an under-emphasised factor of that 2010 election that the finer points of causality were lost on the homeowner electorate. House prices had dipped under Labour, reducing the wealth they might access, and that was enough reason to get rid of them. We've gone from 'It's the economy, stupid' as the main reason to win or lose elections to 'It's house prices, stupid.'

The power and age of this homeowner bloc in many countries have led some to talk about a generational conflict arising from the housing crisis. There has been much talk of 'generation rent', pointing out that a younger generation finds itself losing out to the dominance of the older homeowner bloc. The difficulty of buying a home for younger people has also been given as a key reason for a generation-skewed left wing and failing to follow the Baby Boomers in drifting rightwards as they age. In *Generation Left*,[10] Keir Milburn outlined a strategy by which the left could lean into this generational divide in order to further their politics. Doubtless there is something to the idea that people's politics are determined on aggregate by their relationship to assets (as well as the means of production), and that this is now strongly modulated by age in many rich countries. The older generation were taught to speculate on houses rather than winning better wages, but such a trick could only ever work for a certain amount of time, for it depended on the exploitation of the generations below them. It is easy, then, to imagine a situation of generational conflict, and the popularity of social media memes about Boomers versus Millennials suggests that there might indeed be a generational seismic fault that political entrepreneurs can take advantage of.

But the generational narrative can be misleading, as, of course, many Millennials do get parental help to buy a house, while a renting Boomer has even less chance of saving to buy a house than the renting Millennial. What we are rather seeing is a new dynamic of class stratification occurring through the intergenerational transfer of assets. There is inevitably a racialised element to the stratification too, due to the way class and race intersect in our societies. Questions can also be raised about how many homeowners have truly benefited on balance from the status quo. Many of them might lose their home to pay for end-of-life care because the state has decided to limit its support for the elderly. For those who get into financial trouble, perhaps through illness, or perhaps through mortgaging their house on a business venture, their safety net is suddenly gone. As for their children, if the asset of the house disappears for some reason, they can find themselves economically held back and downwardly mobile. Both generations might have done better with higher salaries and pensions.

TENANT UNIONS STRIKE BACK

One group of people who almost never buy into the generational conflict narrative is tenant union organisers. In part, this is because they want to recruit members in all age groups, and in part because a lot of ordinary people own houses. But it is also because they are focused on a narrower enemy: the landlord. It was clarity about this division between tenant and landlord that led to the birth of perhaps the first tenant union of the new wave of tenant unions, Crown Heights Tenant Union (CHTU).

CHTU emerged when long-term resident organisers, many of them Black women, saw that they needed to work together with young people, some of them former Occupy activists, who were in popular accounts depicted as 'gentrifiers' in Brooklyn, to resist the division that was being sown between them. The real enemy, as the early CHTU organisers saw it, was the landlord, and like labour movement organisers, they saw the need for unity of tenants against the class of landlords. Crown Heights, Brooklyn, had seen its own offshoot of Occupy Wall Street. Like many Occupy activists, once the occupation of public space was over, those involved began to cast around for longer-term projects. Local activists had known for years that many formerly rent-controlled properties were now being let out at market rents. Those who still had rent control, meanwhile, were struggling with building managers and landlord agents whose only interest was to spend as little money as possible and move sitting tenants on. Brooklyn was home to many veteran organisers, many of them Black, many of them tenants in Crown Heights.

So it was that two streams of activism converged, with Occupy activists working together with experienced local organisers to create what would become Crown Heights Tenant Union. At least, this is one way of telling the story: other union members tell it slightly differently, downplaying the role of former Occupy activists, a reminder that the narratives and actions of union are often contested among their own membership.[11] But everyone agrees that people from across the long-term resident/young incomer divide began organising together. They started with a single campaign, against a particular housing brokerage that they knew to be renting out rent-controlled apartments at market rates. In the course of that campaign, as one union organiser describes, they came to realise the pattern of housing issues in the neighbourhood needed to be urgently addressed, for they were seeing issues about: 'immediate displacement, repair and overcharge issues – about, really, the social and ethnic cleansing of the neighborhood'.[12] The organisers decided that what they needed was a dues-paying union structure, originally with some staff support, though the arrangement was later ended due to disagreements with the non-profit providing staffing. Some buildings were already organised into tenant associations, others would get organised with the incentive of a union to support them. These associations formed the base of the union, with the union grouped into locals, and a unifying members' meeting and committee structure to tie it together.

Crown Heights Tenant Union, as its activists see it, is a machine for class and race solidarity in a city that continually tries to pit tenants against each other. It is not natural, in a city such as New York, that older Black women and younger, university-educated white activists work together. But as one activist told me, 'That is what makes it work, that is what solidarity means.' New community is built out of defending blocks from eviction, standing shoulder to shoulder with each other. To build such solidarity is to create the opportunity for the ultimate weapon of the tenant union: the rent strike. CHTU was naturally at the forefront of the rent strike movement during the COVID-19 pandemic in New York, defending its members at their most vulnerable and providing advice to tenants across the city. Despite some misgivings about mainstream politics, parts of the union also involve themselves with lobbying politicians, attempting to get laws changed. CHTU demands reparations for harms done, and a total change to the urban dynamics of displacement. In a 2022 statement it said:

> Landlords push out long-term working class tenants en masse, uprooting Black and immigrant Crown Heights by force, using private-sector muscle called eviction marshals; the same landlords then turn around and illegally overcharge new tenants. The overcharge of new tenants is in no way comparable to the deep harm of displacement of long-term tenants – this cycle is however designed to create a neighborhood and a city for the rich. CHTU builds a union of long-term and new tenants to break this cycle of displacement and overcharge.

Block by block, CHTU is building a power base to counterbalance the forces of gentrification and racial exclusion that to everyone else seem inevitable. That doesn't mean they have all the answers: different parts of the union are still experimenting with different organising methods, trying to increase their effectiveness. They have, however, learnt enough to become an inspiration to thousands of organisers across North America and beyond, helping to plant the idea that the political moment called for a new wave of tenant unions. It is also true that many organisers of new tenant unions may never have heard of CHTU. The never-ending nature of 'housing crisis' meant that in time the idea of tenant unions gained a kind of inevitability. Tenants were suffering, landlords were winning; it was necessary to address the imbalance of power through organising.

Not all tenant unions construct 'landlords' or, if they wish the struggle to be less personalised, 'landlordism', as the main enemy they face down. Other unions are more avowedly anti-systemic in their orientation. In addition, landlords are not the only part of the asset-owning class a tenant union might oppose. Even tenant unions mostly focused on member defence will find themselves fighting a developer where their members are being evicted. Others will see developers, and the entire real estate machinery behind them, as a legitimate target even when they don't directly threaten members. Greater Manchester Tenant Union (GMTU) is one such organisation. According to their lead organiser Isaac Rose, they see themselves as also being a hub from which local neighbourhood conflicts can be fought. One day they might be defending a member from eviction, another day they might be fighting gentrification in the form of a developer knocking down a local vacant pub. Such actions fall into a broad category of actions that aim to 'raise the cost of movement of capital', something that can surely have local effects, and if carried out strategically and at scale could presumably have systemic effects.

But the bread and butter of tenant unions is organising among the main losers of today's housing market: tenants. And this most often means fighting against landlords or their agents. As one union activist put it to me, part of the role of a tenant union is 'trying to politicise the tenant–landlord relationship as an antagonistic dynamic', analogous to a trade union agitating across the boss–worker fault line. This logic leads tenant unions towards trying to construct a 'renter' or 'tenant' subjectivity in the same way that a workplace union will, at its most militant, be attempting to construct a 'worker' subjectivity. The goal of doing that, some organisers might say, is to construct an entire movement of tenants parallel to the movement of workers that is the labour movement.

This is not to say that all of the new tenant union organisers understand the tenant subjectivity in quite the same way. Some with more orthodox Marxist backgrounds will, in line with their belief about the importance of the worker–owner relationship within capitalism, see being a tenant as subordinate to being a worker. In that model of thinking, the tenant subjectivity must build towards a worker subjectivity and be aimed at destroying private property in the means of production as well as in housing. Other tenant organisers have a more nuanced version of that, believing that subjectivities have been successfully disintegrated by capitalism and one must work in the subjectivities of which people feel the most oppressed, or have the most agency to fight back – ideally some combination of the two. Other organisers will simply see being a tenant in itself as the major form of oppression that is worth organising around. Housing is, after all, a site of social reproduction of immense importance, vital to good health, mental health, education and family life. One might even focus on social reproduction itself as the driver that pits tenants against landlords, and wonder if this is something entirely different than the worker–owner dynamic. Other organisers will identify poor tenants in particular (perhaps including the unhoused) as the subjectivity most likely to fight back. All of the organisers agree that the formation of a tenant movement, and implicitly some form of tenant subjectivity, is vital to confront the rolling state of housing crisis in rich countries.[13]

This is no small task, but tenant unions have an advantage on their side: despite the efforts of mainstream economists to make it so, housing is not a tradeable good like any other. Housing is home. Housing means emotional stability. Housing means physical health. It is a necessity as much as water or air. As the main site of social reproduction, it must be functioning in order for other parts of life to succeed, whether work or education or child-rearing. It forms too the building blocks of community, within which wider social reproductive processes take place, and which work best when people can stay in place. It means that people are heavily invested in the idea of home and are prepared to fight for it. As the market/government policy have undermined the ability of people to access a home that is truly affordable and secure, so they have become more willing to fight back. As a necessity of life, not just physically but emotionally, housing therefore becomes one of the key sites of contention of our times.

One person who was prepared to fight was Victoria (not her real name), who had lived for years in a flat riddled with disrepair and vermin problems. Her landlord was a housing association (a non-profit social landlord) now notorious for failing to do repairs in its homes. Her home had damp and mould problems, it had sewage coming back up through the drainpipes, it had exposed electrical wires, maggot infestation, mice in huge numbers leaving droppings everywhere. Like bad landlords all over, the housing association would fail to record her calls to them, would blame her for problems, would lose her complaints, would promise repairs then not deliver, or do only half a job. Years of this squalor, and the failure of the landlord to rectify the problems, had started to affect Victoria's mental and physical health.

But Victoria's instinct that she deserved a safe, comfortable, healthy place to come home to was strong. When she encountered London Renters Union, she joined up, tentatively at first, but when she realised there were people willing to fight alongside her, she threw herself into the fray. The union rapidly escalated the dispute to protests at the landlord's offices, and a social media shaming campaign. Victoria quickly understood the power of the union and encouraged others to join the community she had found. Her victory did not come quickly or easily, but eventually her landlord offered her an entirely new flat in a better-maintained block. It is not easy to get a social landlord to move a tenant when they don't want to, so this was no small accomplishment for her and the union. But there is an emotional importance to home that means people like Victoria, never previously involved in political organising, are prepared to fight.

And despite the difficulty of the fights, the highly entrenched nature of the opposition, and the huge flows of capital opposed to them, tenants can and do get wins, as individuals but more importantly collectively. In late 2022, the City of Pasadena in California passed rent controls into law. The battle to get there had been epic. Tired and angry from the sheer volume of calls about evictions and rent rises that they received on their tenant solidarity hotline, Pasadena Tenants Union had first attempted to get a ballot on the law in 2018 but failed to get enough signatures. Landlords had fought back with their own campaign, well funded and persuasive with dishonest arguments. Pasadena Tenants Union re-mobilised and fought back hard, collecting signatures door to door, phone-banking, working with community organisations, collecting endorsements, and educating people on why it would benefit them to vote for the measure. As ever with such a huge effort, it wasn't only one organisation that made it happen. Many people and organisations pulled together to get Proposition H, as it was known on the ballot paper, across the line. But the Pasadena Tenants Union provided the spine of the campaign, putting the proposition forward and providing much of the organising power.

Now for much of the City of Pasadena rent rises are limited and evictions are more restricted. This makes a real difference to people's lives, enabling them to stay in their own communities rather than being forced out, though it does not allow organisers to sit back and relax: it often takes the pressure of tenant organising to get such laws enforced.

Campaigns like this remind us of something important: whatever the strength of the asset-owning section of society, tenants outnumber landlords by a huge margin. This means that when they get organised, they can win. But the failure of marketised housing to provide people with good homes doesn't inevitably lead to a new era of tenant organising. That is happening because organisers and tenants across the world are taking up the challenge of fighting for their homes. We know that at present most tenants haven't yet joined a tenant union, through lack of opportunity or skills or belief, but joining or starting a union is a choice that any tenant can make. It will take only a sufficiently organised minority of tenants to change the landscape of housing utterly, and tenant unions are the vehicle by which that will happen. The rest of this book will explain in some detail how the new wave of organisation is making an impact, and what victory for the tenant unions might look like.

2

Seizing the Moment

One of the more unusual scenes ever to occur in the plaza in front of the tube station in Stratford, East London, was created by London Renters Union (LRU). One Saturday morning, passers-by found their attention arrested by the sight of a man dressed in a suit bent over with his hands and neck caught in a set of wooden stocks, and a sign round his neck saying 'landlord'. Before him people lined up to take wet sponges from a bucket and throw them at him. People out shopping saw the 'landlord' sign and laughed, many of them stopped, and when encouraged, stepped forward to pick up a sponge. Some did so shyly, others with grim expressions on their face or shouts of anger, their hatred of their landlords shining through. It was not, of course, a real landlord in the stocks. This was an eye-catching LRU recruitment event, and the 'landlord' a long-suffering union member. Having thrown a sponge, willing members of the public were asked to step up to a microphone and talk about how their landlord had wronged them, while others stopped to listen. Around the performance space, a dozen activists stood with forms and phones to sign up new members. The 'landlord' in the stocks not only attracted attention, it drew a visceral response of anger or fear or hatred – and drew in many new members to the union.

The sense of frustration talking to tenants across the world is palpable. If you stand on any street in a big city – and many small towns – of the Global North and ask people if the housing situation is appalling and needs to change, they'll not just say yes, they'll shout it, they'll high-five you as they say it. Selling a tenant union to tenants who have been screwed over is in some ways easy. It's never necessary to argue that something needs to be done, or that the system is skewed against renters. The depths of the problem are all taken as read in the first 20 seconds of the conversation. Most people know in their gut that housing doesn't have to be this bad, for they have experienced better within living memory.

A tenant union needs to argue that it knows the right actions to take to bring about change, and that the potential recruit can play a part in that. Tenants are acutely aware that politicians have repeatedly failed to do anything to improve their situation. To convince them it's worth fighting for better housing, a tenant union has to show that it has a strategy. The creation of a new tenant union *is* a partial strategy in itself. But unions need to demonstrate further aims and strategy to convince new recruits. Across the world political organisers of all stripes have started to see that housing is becoming a touchpaper issue and a rich vein in which to organise. Tenant unions with strategies for winning are what organisers saw they could offer tenants as a way to channel their anger.

The socio-economic landscape that opens the door to tenant unions is the imbalance of power between tenants and landlords. Feeling powerless compared to their landlord fundamentally grates on many tenants. Annoyance soon turns to anger when their attempts to improve their living situation with polite requests get nowhere. It isn't just that their landlord fails to do the maintenance in the first place, it is that all efforts to force them to do the maintenance either seem unwise or turn out to be futile. In a system that prioritises private property over quality of life, it is landlords who have the most power over our homes, not we, the tenants. Into the power vacuum in which tenants as individuals live steps the tenant union, with a strategy, at a minimum, of taking collective action where individual action has failed. As the tenant union demonstrates it can win victories through collectivity, it can grow further. People want to be on the winning side.

However, it is not just any tenant union that can take up the fight in the current landscape. There exists an older generation of tenant unions, particularly in social democratic countries of Europe such as Sweden, France and Germany, but also in parts of the US. These tenant unions tend to be structured such that they mostly help enforce existing rules, offering legal services and keeping rogue landlords in check. San Francisco Tenants Union describes itself as 'fighting for tenants since 1970'. In 1979, as a campaigning union it helped bring rent control to San Francisco. But these days many members join primarily for the thick book of tenant law that is a big part of the service they provide. The union, in common with many other more established tenant unions, also maintains formal relationships with politicians in order to ensure that the rights of tenants continue to be protected. But time has blunted their organisation's once aggressive edge, and what tenants need now is not a union that will uphold the law – which is entirely inadequate – but one that will push well beyond the law in defence of its members.

So it is that we are seeing a new wave of tenant unions, more aggressive, more politically radical, than the older generation. Their distinguishing features are that they will use direct action more than legal routes to defend their members, and that they are explicitly anti-capitalist in political orientation. Some newer foundation-funded tenant unions in the US don't (at least overtly) sign up to this political radicalism and this book will have less to say about them. They are part of a continuous tradition of third sector community organising that is particularly strong in the US. They are an important presence in some cities but are a less recent phenomenon, unlike the more autonomous tenant unions, which are often organised by committed socialists, anarchists and others who want to bring their radical politics to a new style of organising.

TENANTS GET TOGETHER

A couple of years after that recruitment drive in Stratford with LRU, I was part of a small LRU protest heading towards the office of an estate agent. Our member, a woman in her forties, had lived in a property managed by them for some years, during which the agent had failed to do significant and necessary repairs, including to the kitchen, which barely functioned as such. Over the years, the agents had lied to her, ignored her, treated her with contempt, passed responsibility to the landlord, who passed it straight back, and still no repairs were done. It is a feature of housing crisis that no matter how bad people's living conditions may be, they often don't want to move. It costs too much to get a deposit together, you might have to move out of your area, the risk of being turned down by agents is high if your income is low, and if every home within your budget is low quality, you might just be moving out of the frying pan and into the fire. So the LRU member had clung on, but her anger had grown and now she was returning with a union at her back.

As we gathered at a nearby community centre, the member told us her story and spoke of the toll it had taken on her mental health. She thanked us for coming, her eyes brimming with gratitude that we – some of us strangers to her – had turned out for her. She wasn't alone anymore. Then an organiser explained the action and we set out carrying banners with the union's name and slogans, chanting as we walked: 'Here to stay, here to fight, housing is a human right.' As we approached the office of another estate agent that happened to be on the way to our destination, we suddenly saw the shutters go down in a flurry of activity and the office being closed entirely to the public. That agent had been targeted by the union some months previously and now feared they were in for another dose of the union's public shaming tactics. Their reaction of fear to the mere proximity of union members brought joy to everyone at the protest and we moved past their office towards the actual target of the day's protest with renewed energy and excitement. That was the relationship LRU wanted to have with landlords and estate agents: not some cosy, respectable partnership, but to make them live in fear of the union. In the absence of legislation to protect us, how else were we to change the balance of power between tenants and landlords?

When we arrived at the estate agent we were targeting, the owner of the company was outraged that we had turned up at his office and shouted at us for scaring customers away. But, of course, that was the point, and it would take more than a bit of shouting for LRU to back down. The most popular banner as we stood around waiting for him to crumble – and crumble he did, promising to sort out the long-standing problems under threat of a repeat visit to his business – was 'Honk if your rent is too high'. The banner attracted a steady stream of horns, along with thumbs ups and cheery waves from the passing vehicles, underlining that the direct action tactics of the new unions arise not just from the particular politics of organisers but from channelling the anger of members and the public towards the landlords and agents who abuse them.

For activists to think it a good use of their energy to start a tenant union, the anger has to be thick in the air. Housing troubles have to be a common problem of everyday life, and either no tenant union yet exists or an older tenant union is too timid or too embroiled in establishment politics to be of any help. The outrage at the absence of decent housing gradually builds until it feels almost inevitable that tenants get together and organise. The need is so great that it would almost feel wrong not to create a tenant vehicle, the political opportunity so strong that it would feel stupid to miss it. But to understand the deeper political moment that has led to a new wave of tenant unions, we need to look at the wider political landscape. Two streams of political activism have influenced the rise of the new tenant unions, in both their success and their failure.

The first political stream is that arising from what scholars call the New Social Movements that arose in the 1960s. In the new era of mobilisation, activism didn't just take place around workplace issues, and any number of identities might be mobilised in order to fight for new rights or new visions of the world. This stream of activism tried to be very democratic, was often tinged with an anarchist concern with dismantling all hierarchies, and focused on direct action. After various ups and downs through the 1980s and 1990s, this political tendency reached a new peak in the late 1990s and early 2000s with the alter-globalisation movement. For some years, the noise of trade summit protests seemed so loud that it felt like the architects of corporate and financial globalisation would have to listen. Alas, this was an illusory feeling: the meetings to agree trade deals went on, and the outsourcing-plus-cheap goods revolution advantaged or disadvantaged various sections of the population without anyone being meaningfully consulted. In some countries of the Global South, this movement was attached to nationally important movements, but in the Global North the parade of 'summit circuses' turned out to be the same few people – perhaps a few tens of thousands of politically marginal people scattered around the rich countries – who would actually turn out on the streets to try and stop the unleashing of capital by neoliberalism. A widespread accounting of the failure of the alter-globalisation movement was never truly carried out among the activists involved. Between exhaustion and police violence and the war on terror, the summit protests died away. The global financial crash of 2007/8 and the increasing impoverishment of ordinary people in rich countries throughout the first quarter of the twenty-first century would prove the protestors right, but being right in politics is small comfort when you aren't winning.

When Occupy arose then, undergirded by many of the same principles as the alter-globalisation movement (and featuring some of the same people, including such notables as academic and activist David Graeber), not enough questions had been asked of the previous movement to provide any new strategy. Only the tactic of residential occupation of public space was new, with notable camps in New York and London, and a hundred other camps in smaller cities too. In particular, what carried over from the alter-globalisation movement was a determination to be able to critique capitalism without having any duty to propose alternatives. The Occupy camps constituted an exciting and energising moment. The occupiers at Wall Street and St Pauls in the City of London made news around the world, and hundreds of thousands of people experienced the camps in one way or another. For a brief period the taking of space in the core cities of capitalism felt glorious. And then it too died away, with global capitalism very much intact. This time, it had been such a flash in the pan that there was a lot more reflection on what had gone wrong. The ephemeral nature of the camps was now seen by many as too intense an expenditure of energy and time given the lack of concrete outcomes. The failure to make demands, still defended by some, was seen by others as lost potential for change. And the lack of lasting institutions coming out of such a burst of energy made many activists feel depressed and disillusioned. Many swore that next time they would do it differently. One of the founders of Ireland's Community Action Tenant Union (CATU) told me explicitly that they were trying to break a pattern where movements had no infrastructure to help them stay mobilised.

When it came to casting around for new strategies and tactics, the obvious place to look was the other great left tradition: the labour movement and its allied political tendencies. The problem was that this political tradition had also been hitting the buffers. Older organised left parties across Europe had drifted into the 'centre', which over time came to mean being aligned with the right-wing neoliberal consensus. Even newer parties had been chewed up in the jaws of realpolitik. In Greece, the left coalition Syriza attempted to challenge the austerity imposed on Greece after the financial crisis and utterly failed. In Spain, new challenger Podemos, emerging from the *Indignados* movement, Spain's own 'movement of the squares', for a while polled well after the 2007/8 financial crisis, but found it difficult to keep a united front. Eventually, they and related offshoot parties also found themselves stymied by the embeddedness of the neoliberal paradigm.

The neoliberal order stumbled on, zombie-like, regenerating strength with every year that passed after the financial crisis. Everyone had noticed that it was government intervention that had saved capitalism, but those in charge still claimed government intervention was a bad solution to the problems of ordinary people, and a good solution only to the problems and failures of the rich. Many activists, worn out with party political compromises that always saw neoliberalism remain intact, saw the need to build deeper change, to build bases outside of parliamentary politics. What the labour movement tradition could offer to the more left-libertarian traditions of direct action organisations was a focus on building membership organisations, building political solidarity within lasting unions, and creating institutions that could be bearers of resources as well as knowledge.

So it was that many of the new tenant unions drew, like Crown Heights Tenant Union, from both big traditions of the left: hierarchical and anti-hierarchical. In doing so, they aimed to leave behind the strategies that had held both back: being too ephemeral and resource-light, on the one hand, and too at the mercy of leading politicians and backroom deals of the powerful, on the other. The idea of building new membership institutions of the left, but outside of workplaces and with an emphasis on democracy and direct action, was suddenly everywhere. This is not to say that all unions had the same influences – some arose from more specific place-based organising and older community activism currents. But in many cases, tenant unions were a form that brought together in new ways the best of the left traditions to organise around housing as a necessity of life. Their dues-paying

membership organisation model, including some central structures, meant that they were able to shepherd resources that could
be brought to the struggle. Their democratic form meant that they
could be true base-building vehicles. While tenant unions did naturally copy from each other (Ireland's CATU, for instance, initially
modelled itself on LRU), the idea was also emerging in various
places around the world as an answer to the same questions that
everyone was asking about the new strategies needed by the left.
Tenant unions were in the ether, an emergent response to a set
of political as well as housing conditions that had spread across
the Global North. The combination of socialist organising traditions and horizontalist organising traditions converged, through
housing crisis and the instinct to defend home, on the same answer
over and over again, in cities on multiple continents. It was time to
start a tenant union.

FOUNDING MOMENTS

Most new tenant unions are not launched by first-time activists.
Tenant unions are by their nature larger and more complex than,
say, a local anti-gentrification campaign, or being part of an envi-
ronmentalist direct action group. Nearly everywhere a tenant union
has sprung up, it has been launched by a convergence of veterans
of campaigning, protesting and organising. Sometimes the experience brought to the table is truly inspiring, such as the Plataforma
de Afectados por la Hipoteca (PAH) activists who helped set up
the Catalonia tenant union Sindicat de Llogaters, or the Union de
Vecinos activists whose experience of years of struggle in the Boyle
Heights neighbourhood fed into Los Angeles Tenant Union. But
much of the experience founders had was more everyday: activists who had participated in the alter-globalisation movement,
or in socialist organisations, or in local community organising.
Experience was thus brought to new tenant unions from many
political battles, ranging from anti-racist organising through trade
unionism to climate activism.

It can feel intimidating to found a tenant union, because in
doing so the founder members are implicitly making promises to
people: not just that if they join the union will stand shoulder to

shoulder with them in their fights for decent housing, but that they will know how to take on their landlord, and that there is some chance of winning. As soon as a group labels itself a tenant union it is taking up responsibilities to sometimes vulnerable tenants. That doesn't mean that the members joining don't also have responsibilities. Los Angeles Tenants Union likes to say to potential members that if they aren't willing to fight, then they shouldn't expect the union to save them. Solidarity in housing is a two-way street, or rather, a massive multi-road junction going in all directions. But fundamentally, organisers have to be prepared for the reality that once they set up shop, vulnerable tenants will find them and ask for help with difficult situations. Some of those situations might even be so complex and difficult that the tenant has to be told that nothing can be done, or in the case of, say, domestic violence, that the tenant union is not the right group to handle it. A well-organised tenant union has to have processes in place to decide what it can't take on, as well as what it can.

It also takes some planning to start a tenant union, because as soon as it expands beyond organising in one location, the union faces the difficulty of running a networked organisation, and has to make a series of decisions about how to organise itself – whether, for example, it will be very centralised, very decentralised or, as is often the case, somewhere between the two. The union has to be prepared for growth from the outset and have a plan for scaling up. And it has to understand how to run democratic processes in organisations of diverse membership. That's not to say that everyone starting tenant unions is an expert in all of these. Having been involved in founding LRU, I distinctly remember us looking at each other sometimes and admitting that we didn't know how to start a tenant union. Of course, we didn't. We hadn't done it before. Nor had anyone we knew. We were flying by the seat of our pants. In fact, almost no one in the UK had done large-scale radical organising outside of the workplace in our lifetimes. But we had done other organising before, and that made the difference between making elementary organising mistakes and making more advanced mistakes that meant we could still lash the organisation together well enough to get through the initial years.

That doesn't mean less experienced activists have no chance of setting up a tenant union. I met up with organisers for Tenant and Neighborhood Committees (TANC) in San Francisco in 2019 when it was a new organisation just getting started. The activists I met, Democratic Socialists of America (DSA) members, were young and had relatively little experience organising outside of DSA. But the new Bay Area tenant organisation still grew. They learnt from other organisations as they developed. They joined the Autonomous Tenant Union Network (ATUN) to help get ideas and cement their organising. The DSA also has its own Emergency Tenant Organising Committee (ETOC), dedicated to helping DSA activists set up new tenant organisations. With the help of such new networks, it is becoming easier for less experienced activists to start tenant unions. Those networks are also helping tenant unions develop in smaller cities with more limited pools of activists to draw upon, for housing crisis extends not just to big global cities but also to medium-sized and even smaller cities. Tenant unions are growing up not just in Houston but in Austin, not just in Milwaukee but in Madison, not just in Barcelona but in smaller Catalan towns.

But let's go back to the beginning: a tenant union always starts with anger at the current system. Many organisers have personal experience of housing crisis. One founder of LRU told me his story, that of a housing activist who had experienced housing precarity himself:

I moved to London, and I was squatting and got a little bit into the network of people squatting and resisting evictions. And I suppose from there, having been evicted myself, I just really struggled to get myself into secure housing. And I was never street homeless, but actually ... for the first year and a half living in London, I was just moving around a lot, sofa surfing and like that sort of 'hidden homelessness', never being able to get a secure place. And the job that I had ... I was unemployed for a bit when I first moved to London, and then I got a job in a Wetherspoons [pub]. And it was classic gig economy stuff. So it was, you know, not regular hours and like, one penny above the minimum wage. And so it just sort of took me quite a while to get into a place where I was secure in my housing.

A tenant union starts from the frustration that springs from such experiences. It starts too from conversations, between activists and organisers, between organisers and precariously housed people. It begins with 'people are in trouble, they need solidarity', or 'I have trouble with my landlord, why is there no one to help me?' Ideas get thrown around after meetings of other groups, or in a pub or bar in between watching sports. Gradually, a particular idea of what needs to happen starts to coalesce among a particular group of activists.

The need for a tenant union became clear to Barcelona organisers when people approached organisers in the highly successful and politically impactful PAH and asked why they were only helping people who had bought homes. Renters also needed help, it was pointed out again and again. The PAH was set up specifically to help those who had been mis-sold mortgages and were left unable to pay and deeply in debt by the 2007/8 global financial crisis. Its brilliant networked campaigns of direct action had saved many individuals and its political campaigning had won plaudits around the world and helped launch new left parties in Spain. But the ripples of the global financial crisis were now dying away, and in cities like Barcelona it was often those renting who were in most trouble.

Housing organisers in Barcelona, many of whom had been involved in the PAH, or had been involved in squatting and other political action around housing, decided it was time to set up a tenant union. It would be a tenant union that would not only address tenants' specific issues with abusive landlords and high rents, it would also seek to campaign, as the PAH had done, for an entirely new deal for tenants. The Sindicat de Llogaters, as it is called, would start out much like the PAH, inviting tenants into an assembly to talk about their housing problems, relieving them of the shame as well as the stress of bearing their problems alone. Very quickly it developed its ten demands. I include them all here because they say something about the tenor of the new tenant unions:

1. Institute rent controls again and improve how they work
2. All tenant contracts must be automatically renewed (ending no-fault evictions)
3. Ban abuses by estate agents
4. Legislate strict rules around deposits to prevent scams and extra fees
5. Tenants must have a right to unionise, collective bargaining and striking
6. Short-term holiday lets to be returned to the long-term rental market
7. There must be an exponential increase in public housing and affordable rents
8. Empty properties, including those repossessed by banks, must become public housing
9. Landlords must have to offer social rent to vulnerable families in danger of eviction
10. Financial speculation must be ended by legislating its tools out of existence

While any tenant union throughout history wants lower rents and to end abuses by landlords and their agents, we can also sense within these demands a politics that is implicitly, if not explicitly, anti-capitalist. The thrust of several of the points is strongly towards de-marketisation of housing, not just through the mild mechanism of rent control but through stronger mechanisms that insist that private property should be no barrier to housing people. It is in the nature of the new wave of tenant unions that they are anti-capitalist, but it is also in their nature that they don't always talk about their politics explicitly. If one wants to invite all tenants in a city to be members of a union, making it look like an organisation of anti-capitalists would be problematic, for most tenants in any given city are not avowedly anti-capitalist. This does produce some tensions that we will explore later, but it also produces tenant unions far more aggressive than most older tenant unions.

An activist with the Sindicat summed up for me what the union aims to do:

There is obvious inequality driven by housing in Barcelona. Something is wrong when some people can own and others can't, and the laws are always in favour of those that own houses. For five years we've been resisting and winning, we aim to change laws but we don't wait for that, we take action, we organise and we win. We are a pain in the arse to those who want to kick us out of our homes. We are also building a community. We arrive in the union because of a problem, we stay because we want to be in a movement – that can not only transform housing but bring about some sort of revolution in our lifetime.

In the next chapter we will take a longer look at the community-building element of the new wave of tenant unions. Now we will move to the other side of Europe, where LRU likewise grew out of a core of existing housing activists. Many of them had worked together already, either through the organising hub of London's Radical Housing Network or being members of one of its constituent groups. The most significant of these groups was Hackney DIGS, a private sector tenant organisation based in the London borough of Hackney whose organisers eventually decided that what they were doing was too small. They were fighting and winning individual cases but with a base only in one borough of London they felt they weren't big enough to challenge the system. The key activists in DIGS helped to form a group called the Renters Power Project, which morphed into LRU as the decisions about the shape of the organisation fell into place. It would be London-wide, it was decided, it would employ staff organisers so that it could scale up better, and it would be a membership organisation so it could at least partly self-fund. As one founder pointed out at one of the launch events, 'We're not building a new institution for the sake of a new institution. We're really trying to figure out what is required to build renters power.'

Starting out with a focus on the private rented sector, LRU quickly realised that to create real cross-class solidarity in London it needed to do cross-tenure organising. The union began working with tenants in social housing, responding to real needs developing there as council budget cuts meant that maintenance wasn't done, and as supposedly non-profit housing associations became more market-oriented at the cost of neglecting their older properties. Most LRU members are still in the private rented sector but after launch it simply didn't make sense to focus only on private tenants. As one founder member said to me 'We're trying to learn how to organise in a sector that there isn't really a playbook for. That makes it very challenging but also gives us a lot of autonomy and agency.' That agency also meant the organisation would bear the hallmarks of the anti-capitalist activism that many founder members had been involved in. LRU is thus designed to be democratic, inclusive and anti-oppressive, with a strong instinct towards direct action. It is also much bigger than anything anyone involved had done before. Founders were determined that it would contribute not just to housing struggles but to wider left-wing base-building, and to extra-parliamentary movements that could fight against the decades-long rightward drift of Britain's political class.

But all tenant unions start off small; they have to start somewhere. LRU began with only one branch, expanding to three branches later that year. Like the Sindicat de Llogaters in Catalonia, it quickly developed demands that mixed reformist demands with an anti-capitalist thrust:

1. Decent standards in housing
2. Rent controls
3. Indefinite tenancies
4. Housing justice for people living in temporary accommodation
5. No discrimination in access to housing
6. No borders in housing
7. Public housing available to all
8. Housing for people not profit

In a city as multi-cultural and migrant-centric as London, it was perhaps inevitable that one of the main differences between these demands and those of Catalonia's Sindicat is a demand for justice for migrants, or 'no borders in housing'. It was also a response to a specific piece of legislation by the Conservative government with the Orwellian name of 'Right to Rent', which in fact demands that landlords act as border guards and not rent to anyone without documents, on pain of huge fines. LRU always makes the point that housing crisis does not affect people equally, and that those most affected must be at the forefront of the fight.

The elaboration of the final demand is also illuminating: '*End the politics and culture of property as investment rather than to house people, and bring homes into democratic public ownership*'. The union had identified the deeper enemy as capitalism, once again without exactly naming it.

LRU has grown rapidly in the six years since its founding, with some help from the COVID-19 pandemic, which led to a membership boost for most tenant unions. At 7000 members and climbing – making it one of the largest left-wing organisations outside of the workplace in the UK – it is also building an organisation capable of carrying out its mission. The new Labour government in the UK recently announced its Renters Rights Bill, which ends most no-fault evictions, introduces new standards in private rental housing and outlaws several forms of common discrimination by landlords. The bill is an evolution of a long-promised, much-delayed Conservative bill, and it is pressure from LRU and others in the tenant movement that has pushed this government to go further than the previous government.

In the Netherlands, meanwhile, the housing situation was, in theory at least, very different from London's poorly regulated free-for-all. The Netherlands had won rent control some decades previously, and 28.7 per cent of its housing stock is social housing, the highest percentage in Europe. In the UK, the Netherlands is held up as an example of a country that successfully implemented 'second generation rent controls' that had enough flexibility built in to not stymie housing supply in the long term. But Abel Heijkamp of the Bond Precaire Woonvormen (Union of Precarious Tenants, or BPW) described this to me as the 'dying star effect', suggesting that the Netherlands' rent controls are winning attention just as they are being undone. For some time now, many tenants in the Netherlands have been neither protected nor equal. In 2010, the BPW sprang up in response to an increase in precarious tenancies as the Dutch government started to liberalise the housing market. Sold to people as 'flex' tenancy contracts, the flexibility turned out to be, as so often in the case of 'flexible working', almost entirely one-sided, to the advantage of the landlord. But the number of temporary contract types continues to proliferate, and even standard tenancies are becoming more time-limited, and into this gap stepped the union.

BPW started out as a national union, from a network of local working groups who knew their own areas in Amsterdam, Rotterdam, The Hague, Leiden and beyond. To start a new local chapter the union asks only for five active members, making it easy to launch in new cities. The union defines roles that members carry out at the local level to ensure that the chapter functions. What they are fighting is not just the existing 'flexibility' in the rental market but the gradual chipping away of the rent controls put in place in a past, more socialist era. In part, it is facing down neoliberal governments actively undermining the rent controls, but it is also facing creative landlords inventing new non-tenancies in which they claim no 'rent' is paid, yet somehow the fees amount to what looks like a high rent anyway. The more this unwinding of secure tenancy continues, the more potential members the BPW has. The solidarity the union builds means it can not only help members but also plays an important role in calling for protests against the housing situation that attract tens of thousands of people. Tenants in the Netherlands are losing their hard-won housing system, but they are not going quietly, and tenant organisers are determined to win housing security back.

A VARIED ECOSYSTEM EMERGES

Tenant unions, like all social movement organisations that superficially look alike, are founded in a range of flavours and dispositions. Scotland's Living Rent is allied with ACORN International, an offshoot of what was formerly the biggest community organising organisation in the US, and now something of a global network. That means that, while Living Rent has long focused on tenant issues as its name suggests, it has had a lively debate about whether and how to follow the wider ACORN family in expanding their organising to homeowners and non-tenant issues. The organisation is on a journey, having started as more of a campaigning organisation grown out of an Edinburgh tenant activist group, becoming a tenant union only a couple of years later. It now calls itself a 'tenant and community union' and addresses other local issues besides housing. Greater Manchester Tenant Union also began with a structure that looked more like a campaigning non-governmental organisation (NGO). Inspired by other tenant unions, and keen to expand who was involved beyond the 'usual activists', they shifted to a full union structure, ensuring as they did so that staff were subordinate to the elected committee of members.

In Berlin, housing activism is so widespread that the new tenant union has to jostle for position among other campaign and direct action groups. The highly visible Deutsche Wohnen & Co. enteignen (DWE, or Expropriate Deutsche Wohnen) campaign, which successfully lobbied for a referendum to appropriate the properties belonging to large privatised landlords – and won, if not definitively – has dominated international discussion of housing activism in the city, but it is not a tenant union. While tenants of DWE are involved in the campaign, there is no union structure, and the campaign strategy unfolds through centralised meetings. Meanwhile, an older generation of Germany-wide tenant organisations provide excellent legal advice and support to tenants and have large memberships. In recent years, an activist group called Stop Evictions has been living up to its name, perfecting its ability to prevent evictions in Berlin by any means necessary. Even the anti-gentrification campaigning space is taken up with various neighbourhood anti-gentrification assemblies.

The new Berlin tenant union (Mieter*innengewerkschaft Berlin) must find its own space, specifically blocks in which it can form a new base. I went with activists to some blocks being evicted by their pharmaceutical company owner where they were attempting to recruit members. The landlord knows there is a lot of housing activism in Berlin, so they are cunning. People are being evicted in stages, and each time eviction notices are issued, those left behind hope they will be lucky enough to be left alone. The landlord has chosen a strategy that undermines solidarity, and the union finds itself in a tough organising landscape. But organisers think there is space for a tenant union in Berlin and are slowly finding the struggles where solidarity can be built.

In Ireland, the Community Action Tenant Union (CATU) is modelled somewhat after London Renters Union, and has branches across the island of Ireland, operating at a wide range of scales and sizes. Like many tenant union organisers, the organiser I spoke to recognised that CATU are welding together something of a class coalition. They have a lot of young, radical members whose life prospects are worse than their parents – the downwardly mobile, often precariously housed and employed young people who can no longer dream of owning their own home. There is another contingent of long-term housing campaigners from working-class backgrounds, often rooted in council estates where their families have been for a couple of generations now. The final class fraction is recent migrants, more precarious than anyone else, struggling to get on their feet in a country that is often either indifferent or outright hostile to them. There's nothing easy about building such class coalitions, but every tenant union finds it must do so in one way or another. It is the work of building a tenant movement to bring together people whose other life experiences and interests may differ, but who are all suffering under landlordism.

Despite some class fissures and what can seem like a fractured way of operating across different territories, and 1700 dues-paying members, CATU has in fact achieved a significant act of unity that eludes many housing groups: it has come up with a positive vision of what housing in Ireland should look like. Under the name of Universal Public Housing, it proposes the elimination of the private rented sector, and the universal availability of publicly owned housing to all those who don't own a house. The rent would be on a means-tested scale, as it already is in Ireland's social housing sector. To make the vision a reality would require the large-scale seizure of empty properties and properties owned by large landlords, plus a major new building programme funded with the money the government currently doles out to landlords through welfare support for rent. The union's policy statement is unequivocal about their goal:

> Public ownership would mean removing the profit motive from the provision of a basic human need in housing, making it more affordable as one would not have to pay above the odds for the benefit of a private individual or large corporation.

The union also insists:

> This vision is not utopian! Both states on this island have histor-
> ically built public housing on a large scale in the 20th Century,
> and cities like Vienna have over 60% of residents living in public
> housing.

It may not be a utopian vision, but it is a bold one. Most tenant
unions, caught up in the conflicts of the present moment, and keen
to appeal to less radical as well as more radical members, struggle to
articulate anything like this strong, positive vision of what housing
should be. Perhaps it is easier for CATU in part due to Ireland
having had stronger traditions of political organising than much of
the Anglosphere. My bet would be that such a bold vision provides
an advantage in recruitment and campaigning in the long run.

From Vancouver to Seville, from Los Angeles to Dublin, new
tenant unions are springing up. They willingly take on an enormous
challenge, for they are emerging in a political landscape in which
traditions of big organising outside of electoral organising have
largely been lost, and organising outside of workplaces in particular. Tenants, along with everyone else, have been pummelled for
decades by and with a largely top-down-imposed individualistic
culture. They have little experience of solidarity, might even sneer
at the use of the word. They inhabit highly stratified and atomised
societies in which people not only don't talk to people outside their
social class, they often don't even talk to their neighbours.

One of my first experiences of housing activism was doing a
community consultation about a proposed development by the
local council which, rather than building council housing, was to
offer only private rented sector properties. Two things struck me
while talking to people on the doorstep. The first was that, while
most people agreed that the development sucked, most people felt
entirely hopeless about challenging those in power. They told me
to my face that we would lose, because ordinary people always
lose. The second striking discovery came from the inclusion in the
questionnaire of a question about people's links to any collective or
participatory activities in the local area, whether church, mosque
or local park improvement society. The vast majority of people, it

turned out, had no such links at all. Their whole worlds consisted of friends and family. It is the duty of an organiser to link these two findings: people feel that they will always lose precisely because they are not part of any larger collectives.

The mission of the new tenant unions then is to not only take on the vast, rolling, global housing crisis arising from neoliberal policy, but to reconstitute communities that have been plundered and divided by neoliberalism. They have to show that collectivity can win victories where individualism fails, and they must do so in a cultural landscape that lionises individualism in the form of rise-and-grind culture more than ever before. It is a testament to the tenacity of organisers that so many new tenant unions have emerged in so many cities around the world. Cross-class, cross-racial organising in such a landscape is no easy task, and the next chapter is dedicated to discussing how tenant unions address the challenge.

3

Organising Communities

I arrived at the meeting point on a grey day in southeast London, with rain threatening. The residents of a council-owned block were coming out to protest under-investment in the block. This had resulted in chronic disrepair and major security problems, with the corridors and stairwells of the maze-like complex becoming crime hotspots. Thirty or so residents showed up, some of them with children in tow. They held banners and placards they had made themselves: 'We deserve better homes', 'Enough is enough' and 'Fix our homes'. At first they were quiet and seemed shy, but then a London Renters Union staff member started up a chant of 'We deserve better, enough is enough', taking his cues, it seemed, from the placard slogans the residents had chosen. Within a few minutes, we were 40 people, and we all started out in the direction of the council offices. A couple of people unfurled an LRU banner. I helped give out leaflets to passers-by about an upcoming LRU community meeting, and struck up conversation with residents.

After hesitating a few times about the route, we arrived at the front door of the council's housing office, chanting and waving placards. A local LRU member had brought a small sound system and people began to speak on the microphone about their experiences, or just took the mic to shout demands that the council's cabinet member for housing come out and talk to us. Others took the mic to lead chants such as 'Housing is a human right, here to stay, here to fight'. Two of the people who spoke were the main leaders among the residents of the block. One of them, an older man of Caribbean origin, asserted the humanity of the residents by shouting 'We are not animals.' Another resident said that everyone deserved housing as nice as the council's Head of Housing, to loud cheers. 'I'm sure you're not living in housing like us!' the resident shouted. A couple of LRU staff organisers also spoke, though their usual role of stirring up the crowd seemed almost unnecessary in the face of the residents' own exhortations.

Eventually, a housing officer came down and a quiet conversation was held with a few of the residents. Then an LRU staff organiser got the microphone and explained that we had won a victory: the cabinet member for housing would come to the negotiating table in a few weeks' time. They would listen to the residents' concerns and had promised to do everything they could to help. The staff member repeatedly said, 'We should celebrate what we've achieved here today,' and the crowd slowly stopped chanting, then began to whoop in victory. With a display of unity and strength we had achieved what we had set out to do that day. Within months the council would spend hundreds of thousands of pounds repairing the neglected block.

This type of protest, attended by people who had never been to protests before, of diverse backgrounds and migration status, is only made possible by organising. By necessity in a city like London, this means cross-class, cross-racial organising. That doesn't happen by accident, and most tenant unions have some way of describing what they do that encompasses what they believe about organising and how to do it. LRU drew in activists and staff who had a particular interest in what one staff member described as 'building grassroots power' through radical community organising. In the US, the term 'community organising' has been so defined by a particular organising methodology promoted by Saul Alinksy that many radical organisations are wary of using the term, even if on some level what most tenant unions do is organise communities. In particular, Alinskyite community organising tends to repudiate 'politics', attempting to simply focus on what 'communities' want – though in reality Alinsky's own organising was openly anti-communist. It also generally happens through existing community institutions, often churches, with existing community leaders recruited and leveraged to increase the power of the organising.

But in the UK, the term 'community organising' has far less baggage attached to it. Historically, the term has been little used, with only one major national Alinskyite organisation, Citizens UK, explicitly referring to what it does as community organising. That is why organisations like LRU are happy with defining what it is they mean by community organising, even if they feel the need to add the qualifier 'radical' to it. ACORN UK, like its originator organisation in the US, uses similar terminology, referring to themselves as a 'community union' that does community organising. For ACORN as a whole, the use of the term 'community organising' reaches back to its founding in the 1970s, when there was a more widespread feeling among organisers in the US that community organising could be radicalised. I will mention ACORN UK a few times in this book because in the UK they were for a few years calling themselves a 'tenant union'. Internationally in the Global North, they have generally called themselves a 'community union', and in the Global South, they have mostly organised in informal settlements. In the UK, they have now followed their international colleagues in calling themselves a community union, but a large part of their caseload and campaigning still addresses tenant issues.

The question of which organising methods to use, and the desire to call on methods of the past or from other continents, arises from the particular political situation many organisers in rich countries have found themselves in. From the 1980s onwards, traditions of political organising had been in decline, both in workplaces and outside of them. I came to political maturity in London in the early 2000s, by which point political organising in the UK was an extremely niche activity. Very few people of my generation defined themselves as 'left wing', and politics rarely even came up in conversation. Anyone who brought it up (as I did) tended to attract odd looks. Politics was all so passé. Through the neoliberal period since the 1980s, including the swing of formerly left parties to neoliberalism, a thoroughly de-politicised culture had settled over many countries. That meant that when people began to establish tenant unions in the UK, and in many other places, they did so in a context in which the left traditions of collective action had fallen out of collective memory. Barely anyone knew how to do organising at all, let alone extra-parliamentary organising outside of the workplace. Tenant unions had to search wherever they could to find organising tools that they could rework to their own ends.

Both LRU and ACORN UK have a particular spin to their community organising: they create new communities through organising, rather than organising through existing communities like Alinskyite organising, or like a lot of the informal settlement organising in the Global South. This is not a defining feature of tenant unions and some of them do organise through existing communities. But the organising landscape in the UK is such that LRU's form of community organising was almost inevitable. Unlike in the US and many other countries, it is unusual for British people to belong to a church or religious institution that they regularly attend. Community life more widely has been so shattered by waves of capitalist innovation/destruction that it often feels like, outside of certain well-organised migrant groups, there is little in the way of existing community to start from. This has the consequence that in order to be a diverse union, LRU had to do organising from scratch, door to door, or more commonly on street stalls such as the one described at the beginning of the previous chapter. Like any new tenant union, LRU's 'unintentional' recruitment happens through networks of left-wing activists, but to fulfil its ambition of having a diverse membership that reflects the population of London's renters, LRU has no choice but to go out on the streets and find people where they are.

Organising on the street and door to door – organising the unorganised – is undoubtedly a slog. It is the nature of our de-politicised, individualistic society that more people will ignore than take up what the union is offering. To help its members carry out this challenging work, LRU trains people in having organising conversations. It has used various models for these conversations over the years, including the LAVA model. This acronym describes the four stages of an organising conversation: Listening, so as to understand what problems the person faces; Agitating, by asking questions such as 'Who is benefitting from this?'; explaining a Vision, or plan to win; and finally asking the person to take an Action, which might be as simple as coming to the next branch meeting near their home.

But it is the next step on which LRU has worked the hardest: creating local branch meeting spaces that feel accessible and welcoming to everyone. Part of this ethic of inclusivity is about helping people solve practical problems that would prevent them from getting to meetings: providing childcare, providing food in the meeting so they don't have to cook that night, providing language interpretation where necessary. But part of it too is about creating a space in which someone who isn't a political activist can feel comfortable. No political expertise is necessary to take part in an LRU branch meeting, only a visceral understanding that better housing must be fought for. Even if someone expresses a right-wing view, such as blaming immigration for shortages of council housing, they might be gently corrected and someone have a quiet chat with them about it in the break, but they won't be shamed for it. It is understood that people come to the union with vastly different experiences and levels of political understanding. Part of what the union wants to do is help people move forward in their political understanding of the world, and that won't happen by pouncing on every mistake they make and making new members feel uncomfortable.

The final factor in making the branch meeting spaces welcoming for everyone is LRU's ethos of employing paid organisers, who have the time to nurture and mentor people who aren't used to being in organising spaces. This will mean work outside of meetings as well as in them, perhaps asking a newer member to take on some simple element of running a branch meeting so that the space starts to feel like theirs. Building the confidence of people who wouldn't normally participate in meetings is time-consuming but absolutely key to a union that can work across race and class lines. The union describes this as 'leadership development' as is common in community organising, but with the proviso that what the union aims for is a 'leaderful' movement, not one in which particular people dominate.

Another key part of LRU's strategy is having a rolling programme of training events for its members. It has three major types of training events that it offers, the first being a new member training that encourages new joiners to engage in the union from a position of understanding its goals. The second is 'member solidarity' training which is offered to those who want to help run the peer support processes for members in housing crisis, with training in everything from renters' rights to how to get members to lead their own housing cases. The third is 'organiser training' for more involved members, and this teaches LRU's version of community organising. It is run every few months, with the training of members in organising being one of the key goals of the union.

LRU organising trainings draw on everything from ordinary community organising tools such as one-to-one meetings, through facilitation skills drawn from horizontalist social movements, to consciousness-raising literature. LRU tries to offer anyone involved in the union the chance to go to training events that will draw them further into the organising of the union. Where training spaces are limited, priority will be given to members from marginalised groups, but the training of its young, university-educated, 'middle-class' members is also important.

As an aside, I will often put 'middle class' in inverted commas throughout the book, because I don't believe that the common usage of it for all university-educated people always makes sense – many university-educated people in rich countries now have a relationship to the means of production and to assets that places them in the working class, if sometimes in a hybrid way. That said, class divisions even between fractions of the working class are real, and it is important to avoid constructing a 'working class' that consists only of those who are usually called 'middle class'. What LRU is doing is creating a space of encounter between people who don't usually mingle with each other. For many 'middle-class' members it will be the first time they've ever mixed with people from very low-income groups, and it's important that they act in a way that empowers those members rather than makes them feel inadequate.

LRU sees this space of encounter between people of different class and racial backgrounds as one of the key goals and achievements of the union. One staff member explained to me:

> As time has gone on, I have really seen first-hand the power of bringing people together from a range of backgrounds on the topic of housing. And I find the combination of building power behind radical ideas and also supporting people to win material improvements to their lives – that's a really exciting combination for me.

Housing, like any part of our social and economic worlds, is highly stratified in how people experience it. Only a diverse union can fully understand the extent of housing problems, and the need for housing solutions. More than that, the purpose of a union is to empower those who have little power standing alone. That means recruiting those members who need a bit more work to bring them on board, not just those who have an instinct to join political organisations. This results in a rare type of community – or set of communities, since different branches or chapters might produce different organising according to local demographic makeup – with the knowledge, passions and life experience drawn from a wide variety of people. Does this make for a better fighting union? Almost certainly, but LRU and many other unions would choose to do it anyway, for organisers adhere to the principle that a union that doesn't uplift the weakest in society isn't worth the trouble of building. It is also rewarding in its own right, as a staff member pointed out to me:

> I think that this work of creating communities where they don't exist is actually really cool. I think it's really amazing how you see people connecting with each other and supporting each other and really coming together who would otherwise really not. You'll see people [neighbours] start, like, talking to each other in daily life.

Of course, the community, once it is brought into being, also has to build power, and that element of union-building will be discussed further in the next chapter.

FROM ACTIVISM TO ORGANISING COMMUNITIES

All of the new British and Irish tenant unions do 'community organising' in some form or another, deploying the classic tools – one-to-one meetings between organisers and members, identifying commonalities, building local groups, leadership development and base-led campaigning – that characterise the community organising approach. They are using the community-*building* approach rather than working through existing community institutions, partly due to the previously mentioned low level of community and religious engagement in the UK (what civic engagement does happen is largely carried out by those on higher incomes), and partly due to the landlord–tenant divisions within existing communities. In a country with two million landlords it would not be unusual for the leaders of a church or mosque to be landlords. But CATU, GMTU and Living Rent identify with this approach as much due to the political mood of the times as anything. Some housing organisations such as London's Housing Action Southwark and Lambeth do much of what a tenant union does, but they don't describe themselves as doing community organising. They evolved slightly earlier, when a more avowedly anti-hierarchical politics was more widespread. While their members are largely tenants and they do form a community, they would see 'community organising', labelled as such, as descended from too hierarchical a tradition to want to use the term.

The grassroots political landscape has not shifted entirely away from anti-hierarchical politics, so all of the tenant unions also strive to be democratic and bottom-up. This can create a tension with the desire that some tenant unions express to move away from 'activist' ways of doing things, an ambition that reflects their understanding of 'activism' as a minority, even subcultural activity. LRU uses a rough version of consensus decision-making and for most 'non-activist' recruits it will be the first time they have encountered such a process. It can work well sometimes, but when a lot of time gets burned up on decision-making in meetings it isn't uncommon to hear mutterings from some members about the union being 'a bit too democratic'. Tenant union organisers have to balance the desire for the kind of democracy they have experienced in activist groups with the culture shock this can create for new arrivals.

The Irish tenant union CATU has tried to move further than most away from their 'activist' roots. In as far as they want to be influenced by other traditions, they seem to prefer radical trade union organising as a model, with their introductory booklet quoting at length some 1980s advice to organisers from the US trade union, Service Employees International Union (SEIU). When I spoke to one organiser, they emphasised their ambition to structure union activity such that it isn't so centred around meetings:

The big focus of the union is actually just: identify issues, plan actions around them and limit the number of meetings. So the first thing they might come to [after joining and getting a phone call from an organiser] is actually an action. Not a meeting. Or increasingly we're trying to diversify and not have meetings. Other ways to get to chat to more people are, like, you might have a coffee morning or a social or something like that. That's kind of accessible, but the folks will be getting towards an action as soon as possible – and into a role. If the organisers are prioritising that area, and are putting extra resources in, we'll chat more about their issues and how they can slot in and what skill they have to particularly contribute. If it's something small, and you might have someone who wants to do a bit of graphic design, and can't go to actions, we'll try to get them on that as soon as possible, like a tangible task. So the tangible tasks and actions is the focus now.

Even though CATU learnt a lot from LRU at its launch, this approach is rather counter to LRU's one of building the branch meeting as the most important community space of the union. While LRU sees the nature and inclusivity of that space as being their step away from 'activist' ways of doing things, for CATU the avoidance of meetings is their conscious effort to break from old ways. But according to the same organiser, it has not yet permeated the union entirely:

Some groups do a monthly meeting that's, like, two hours, and don't do an action and then do a housing case and then do a social media post and then do another meeting. But we do discourage that. You know, pockets of that culture have carried over from past organising experience or from leftist activism. But yeah, it's kind of not our model. I want to see one-hour meetings max, with a clear purpose.

Some tenant unions would doubtless find this approach to minimising meetings too strong, perhaps even compromising democracy or relationship-building or critical reflection, but it illustrates well the types of debates that unions have had internally about how to build community, how to be accessible and how not to fall into 'left activist' ways of doing things that others might find alienating. What radical 'community organising' represents to British and Irish tenant unions, among other things is finding ways to break out from activist subcultural modes of behaviour in order to become truly broad-based unions.

AUTONOMOUS COMMUNITY

Now we will move across the Atlantic and across the whole continental US, to the West Coast where another tenant union is also organising communities, if in a rather different context. Los Angeles Tenant Union (LATU) on the face of it looks like a similar organisation to London Renters Union. They would not generally use the term 'community organising' for what they do because of the particular history of that term in the US, but like all tenant unions they do organise communities. The first sign that LATU is something of a different beast to the unions I was familiar with in the UK came when I attended one of their meetings in Los Angeles and saw the simultaneous interpretation between English and Spanish in action. While in LRU, there will sometimes be an interpreter sitting with one or two members helping them through the meeting, in LATU, Spanish is a common enough language that they have created a hardware infrastructure of mics and WiFi headphones, along with enough willing translators, to ensure that most meetings can be thoroughly bilingual. Now with 'more than ten' locals – organisers said it could be hard to quantify the number of locals as there are always new ones springing up, some of which succeed, some of which don't – LATE is spreading across the city.

LATU's specific language to describe their organising of communities is of a process of 'base members organising themselves'. The base members are those most impacted by the violence of gentrification, organising out of tenant associations formed within blocks. The union strategy emerges from their experience and during a 2022 're-founding' process that tried to ensure that it is genuinely steered by the base, the union affirmed itself as having four main goals:

1. Learning together for empowerment
2. Women organizing community defense
3. Building relationships as security
4. Retaking our space

The first goal reflects the roots of LATU, coming as it did out of a radical education collective inspired by the militant pedagogy that elements of the left often fruitfully rediscover when they are struck by the awareness that they don't, in fact, have all the solutions for the problems of poor people. The second goal that union organisers pointed out to me is simply the union becoming aware of who its base is: mostly Latina women. This reflects the fact that Los Angeles has a high migrant population from Latin America, vastly outnumbering other migrant populations, and in fact the largest ethnic grouping in the city. It also reflects the fact that in most places in the world, most housing organising is done by women: there is an under-theorised link between the realm of social reproduction and housing organising.

I asked organisers about the third goal, 'Building relationships as security': what is the notion of security being used here? It turns out that it means more than housing security. It means developing communal aspects of living, an 'intimacy of economic life', being able to count on one another, not just in housing, but for food, childcare and so on. One of the organisers points out that:

> People live in fear, like tremendous amounts of fear. And so the idea of security is, what will counter that fear? Will we get to it by answering people's questions about what rights they have? No, we get to it by people knowing that they have relationships and that they know that there's a kind of ... there's a network of people that they can depend upon.

The organiser is explicitly making the point that LATU exists not just to advise people on tenant rights, which had historically been the focus of the 'activists' of the union. The union now sees itself as more than a tenant union, more than just a housing organisation. The union's fourth goal clarifies that the union is about more than just 'tenant rights'. Are the places people occupy forever to be thought of as belonging to the landlord? The union rather imagines a concept of ownership established by tenant action and sociality, spaces occupied as home belonging to those who live there. This is one of the reasons the tenants will always invite the landlord to meet in the building rather than at the landlord's office. The landlord must experience the fact that the building is the tenants' territory, while the tenants experience their own power in their home space.

LATU also brings a distinctive flavour to its organisation of/ with communities. It does not employ any staff, including any paid 'organisers', and it has an almost autonomist disdain for electoral politics, encouraged by the Democrat machine politics of Los Angeles that sees city, non-profits and unions alike committed to gentrification. LATU sees itself more as preparing for an age of climate and other disasters in which the state is likely to withdraw more and more, leaving people unprotected. The social parts of organising are emphasised as vital, with a recognition that social life already exists within the buildings in which their tenant associations grow. As one organiser explained:

> One of the ways some of us have tried to conceptualise the tenant association is on a continuum between the social life of the building and a political struggle. And the tenant association 70% of the time is the intentional organisation of the social life in the building. And only like 10%, max 20% of the time, is actually the intentional political struggle.

The role of 'middle-class' activists in this vision is to make sure that learning spaces happen, rather than to express their own politics too loudly. In those spaces, activists/organisers from all backgrounds can have a pedagogical role, described by one organiser as 'posing questions that then the group wrestles with, not over the course of one meeting, but on a regular basis and in multiple situations or contexts'. Radical pedagogy in the traditions of Brazilian educator Paolo Freire forms a part of the everyday practice of the union.

This pedagogical practice comes out most strongly in the way LATU ensures it is strategically orienting itself according to the needs of its base. It has developed a process it calls 'tenant inquiry', which models itself on the 'workers inquiry' developed within Italian autonomism as a process of self-discovery and strategy development for workers. 'Workers inquiry' was a process of workers questioning each other, perhaps with some input from movement intellectuals, moving slowly towards understanding of their own position in labour processes and therefore of their power. Likewise, 'tenant inquiry' is a process by which tenants come to understand their position, their power, and where power can be built and space taken in the future. LATU creates spaces for constant learning to happen between members, but has also progressed their tenant inquiry through interviews with members, listening exercises, and through analysing together the contradictions that emerge. The collective analysis can then lead to another round of collective learning and debate, and so on, through multiple cycles of learning. Through the iterative process members learn about themselves and about what they are doing. One member said that she was struck by the realisation – that had only been put to her in her inquiry interview – that 'we are women supporting each other. Once someone said it to me, I was like, *oh yeah, that's what we're doing*'. This is community-building as consciencisation, or perhaps consciencisation as community-building.

LATU is pioneering a model for tenant organising that prioritises building power from the base. This approach doesn't simply empower existing communities; it actively cultivates them into politically engaged forces, based within their social worlds. A member who took part in their tenant inquiry expressed how LATU sees community in relation to tenant organising:

One of the things I love about our little community, all these people who live here, is that we have always, it's just the kind of people we are, we always have looked out for each other. You know, if I hollered out the window, I know somebody would come. That's how we have always been. And that's how the world … you know, that's the kind of world I want to live in. And sometimes you can be that way, but unless you have a name for it, like tenants association, or neighbourhood group or something like that, other people don't realise that that's how you are, and unless people – other people – realise that, it can't become contagious, it can't grow past that and more people can't believe that we can live like this.

Thus, the link between pedagogy and community-building becomes clear: through radical learning processes people can become more aware of both how they live now and how they might live. This is LATU's version of communities organising themselves.

Naturally, this learning in LATU must all happen alongside and through the everyday work of the union: preventing evictions, forcing landlords to do repairs and building new tenant associations, all the work of fighting for 'dignified housing'. It is worth noting that their everyday struggles take place in a city that has rent control and 'just cause' statutes to limit evictions, yet the housing people inhabit is still unaffordable and security of tenure must still be enforced by collective action. The immediate practical work is always intertwined with the pedagogical work in communities. One organiser told me that many of their members on low incomes had become used to doing their own repairs. They are skilled labourers or they know skilled labourers, so practically speaking it is often easier to get a leaking pipe sorted out through friends and relatives than through pursuing the landlord to fix it. But over the years, the cost of this mounts up, and the bigger, more structural repair work never gets done. The pedagogical work is to help members see how the power relations between tenant and landlord have pushed tenants into doing their own repairs, and how, by getting together, the tenants can reverse the power relationship and force the landlord to fix their buildings. It might also involve encouraging the tenants to make decisions between themselves, such as one case where the landlord prevaricated over allocating parking spaces and the tenants simply took it into their own hands to organise parking in a way that suited them.

For LATU this is about better housing but it is about far more than that: it is about resilient communities that can organise themselves in the face not just of landlords but of the coming economic and political failures that globalisation and climate change have made inevitable. While some tenant unions do long-term base-building in the hope of wielding power in electoral processes,

LATU does long-term base-building for a future of greater mutual aid. They are offering their methods to other tenant unions across North America through the Autonomous Tenant Union Network, so this may become a more widespread model in the coming years – or at least we can expect other tenant unions to borrow tools and methods from LATU's well-elaborated organising methodology.

JOINING STRUGGLES TOWARDS NEW SOCIETIES

In Barcelona, meanwhile, political organising happens in a wildly different context to Los Angeles. An obvious difference is that there are some meaningfully left-wing parties to vote for and a hope of at least social democratic policies that can improve people's lives. But arguably the more important difference is that Barcelona is one of the most politically organised cities in Europe, possibly the most organised. While visiting the Sindicat de Llogaters in Barcelona, I was struck by the wide array of spaces available to social movements across the city. The busy record of long-term left-wing organising and independence movement organising in recent decades has left its mark in the very fabric of the city, with community-controlled spaces far more common than in my own City of London. This environment has had a major impact on the trajectory of the Sindicat's organising with communities, for the communities are often already organised.

At the outset, the Sindicat had a clear ancestor to follow: they could model themselves on the PAH, the organisation that spread across Spain to help organise mortgage-holders affected by the country's economic collapse following the 2007/8 financial crisis. Like the PAH, they set up an assembly to which tenants could come, discuss their housing problems and there discover that they were not alone and there was nothing to be ashamed of, for they were victims of systemic problems and not their own moral failings. With the input of organisers this could then be built into a process of supporting each other, building solidarity and moving towards campaigns. From their experience in the PAH they knew that, with time and organising, a community of tenants could be formed with the stomach for fights against landlords, and against governments and authorities who had left tenants to fend for themselves.

There was nothing wrong with that model in itself, and in other parts of Catalonia other branches of the Sindicat were following the formula with success. But Barcelona is a big city, so after some time of meeting fortnightly and the meetings getting longer and longer, the organisers realised that so many people were coming that it couldn't be sustained. They switched to weekly meetings to be able to work with more tenants in crisis but, particularly after the pandemic hit, this still wasn't sufficient to cope with the numbers of tenants who needed help. The density of organising that already existed across the city meant that it wouldn't have made sense to create a new network of assemblies either. Instead, while maintaining the central assembly, the Sindicat has also built relationships with existing neighbourhood unions (*sindicats de barri* or *d'habitatge*) that address a whole range of local issues, from fighting gentrification to organising rent strikes in apartment buildings. Those local unions are membership organisations, so where the Sindicat de Llogaters has affiliated with the unions, their members also become members of the Sindicat. This means the Sindicat de Llogaters is able to build on community organising that has been embedded in place for years, offering mutual aid to tenants through politically sympathetic communities and networks that already exist.

The Sindicat de Llogaters has a handful of paid staff who help do some of the work necessary at the centre of the union. This mid level of staffing is enough to make sure the organisation keeps running, with paid staff doing some organisational work behind the scenes, plus plugging gaps when 'volunteer' members are unable to complete tasks they've taken on. They represent a middle point among the options for staffing strategies, while London Renters Union has moved towards higher staffing, now approaching 15 staff members. LRU wants to employ as many organisers as possible on the grounds that cross-class, cross-racial organising is incredibly time-consuming. But doing community organising without staff at all is also possible. Los Angeles Tenants Union and Crown Heights Tenant Union both operate without paid staff.

Most tenant unions with no staff do have a committed core of people who, due to their personal life situations, are able to commit substantial amounts of time to the union. I will discuss staffing strategy options in much more depth in Chapter 5, but I raise the issue here because it touches on the question of how difficult it is to organise in/with communities in our atomised societies. Or is it difficult? Los Angeles Tenants Union organisers say that if organisers are embedded within communities – whether those they originate in or those they have chosen to accompany – then it shouldn't be so difficult. If the organiser is part of the community, they are nourished by it as well as giving to it. In Los Angeles, it may also be a factor that Latin American communities, coming as they do from more communal cultures, more easily organise themselves than more individualistic groups in the US. Community often already exists and only needs to be coaxed towards greater awareness of its own power. Building community where there is virtually none at all, as in much of London, is an intimidating task and it is not surprising that many tenant unions see the need for staff organisers.

As an aside, outside of the community-building approach it can actually be easier to do housing campaigning with few or no staff. The highly impactful Berlin DWE campaign, calling for the expropriation of privatised rental properties, operated across all of Berlin with only one person paid part time. The key to their ability to project themselves into the political sphere was that they were not trying to organise communities. They were doing mobilising rather than organising and so could act quickly and sharply. Mobilising work is less deeply embedded in communities and less time-consuming. The campaigner might be asking people to sign a petition or turn up to one or two protests. There's no need to develop long-term relationships and so it is easier to run the campaign on volunteer time. While we won't detour further into this approach here, it is worth highlighting that there are strategic moments and situations in which mobilising may have higher impact than deeper organising. But almost invariably this will be about shorter-term effects. Most of the new tenant unions are concerned with the long-term effects of their organising, while naturally eager to also take any short-term wins that might be available.

It is important to note that most of the tenant unions mentioned so far have quite specific long-term political outcomes they see as desirable. They all want to see the undoing of the effects on society of 40 years of neoliberalism. In a world that has built itself around relentless competition, tenant unions have decided that the 'losers' in that competition matter. In a world that has valued or pretended to value 'equality of opportunity', while in reality economic stratification has become deeper and deeper, tenant unions want to propagate actual equality. In a world that has constructed migrants as a servant underclass, tenant unions want to increase the political agency of migrants. As quality of life declines in many rich countries, the message of 'There Is No Alternative' has been internalised, and political struggle replaced with a hustle and grind culture that individuals are taught to see as the solution to their financial instability. Tenant unions respond with an intention to teach again the meaning of solidarity, not on paper but through action. They arise in a context where the visible actual failures of neoliberalism in a global financial crisis have done nothing to undo the institutions of neoliberalism or its dominance as a governing mentality. It is now abundantly clear that crises of capitalism don't automatically result in change. People must be mobilised on a large scale to ensure that crises can lead to positive change. Tenant unions are one way of preparing for the next crisis.

As we have seen, however, the focus of tenant unions is not just on what they must fight but on what they can create. To build a new community is to change lives, one's own as an organiser and the lives of other people. In my experience, organisers don't often focus on or discuss the individual experience of community-building, since the main purpose of it is to build collective power. But having done the work of community organising myself, there is something important about the processes that one goes through as an individual becoming an organiser. A city like London prides itself on its diversity but it can be easy for people to move around the city (or sometimes stick in one place) entirely within their own socio-economic and cultural strata. The diversity is there, and yet a *de facto* segregation still operates as most Londoners sort themselves by income level, by food culture, by language preference.

In LRU, culturally 'middle-class' (and a few genuinely middle-class – the children of successful business owners, for example) university graduates mingle with low-income working-class people for the first time, and come to understand the lives of those who do the undervalued work in our society. Working-class people mingle with middle-class people and learn skills that will help them fight back against bureaucracies and institutions that exercise power over them. Phrased like that it might sound a little transactional, but I can say from experience that most of the relationships are not so. Friendships and affinities form, new connections emerge between people who society has largely kept apart. Some members of LRU, most from migrant backgrounds, have said to me that they feel the organisation to be their family. They may not be friends with everyone in their branch, but they know that their union has their back.

The hope of the new tenant unionism lies in the power of diverse communities coming together. This means members actually sitting down together, listening to each other, learning how to struggle for housing and support each other. The unions can be seen as laboratories developing new knowledge and strategies for social movements. Over time, more and more people will have experiences of collectivity that will transform their relationships to the world and each other. Over time, such communities will develop political experience together, leveraging community into power. This is the ultimate end of any radical organising of communities, and wealthy countries with poor populations need many more people building that power. It takes genuine work to organise beyond one's own social strata, but there are so many rich relationships to be formed along the way that I apologise to no one for suggesting that they get out there and do it. It is vital that within this organising, no great division is allowed to appear between key activists and more marginalised 'base members', for in that division much of the radical possibility of tenant union evaporates. Thus, a successful union has a social life as well as a political life. Consciously building communities of solidarity will change your life for the better, it will change the lives of others for the better, it will change the political landscape. This is how tenant unions present a challenge to neoliberalised society: it is the sociality as much as the idea of housing justice that it is so bursting with potential.

Some of this could be said about radical trade unionism too, but it is vitally important to do such organising beyond the workplace.

One of the features of trade unions of yesteryear that is often forgotten is that they were based in communities. Today, to go to a large employer the workers will drive or get the train from miles around; they constitute no sort of community at home. In the past, people not only worked alongside each other, they lived alongside each other too. The evening union meeting could happen in the local pub or a neighbour's house, and most had only a few minutes' walk to join it. The days when factories were surrounded by their workers' homes are probably gone forever in most of the Global North (though not in the Global South). Perhaps never again in rich countries will workplace organising be so centred in geographic communities. Something important is lost forever; the community-based element of trade union organising that may have been a key to its success has simply evaporated. Today's trade unions can fight neoliberal impositions of wage cuts and lost benefits in the workplace, but it is hard for them to fight *for* a positive community of the kind that used to form through labour organising. At the end of the working day everyone goes home, often to different towns. While there have been half-hearted efforts to correct for this – in the UK, the large conglomerate union Unite has tried with limited success to set up community branches – I suspect that trade union organising will never quite get over the loss of geographically localised community around workplaces.

A tenant union, on the other hand, is naturally based in the places where people live. It can bring the experience of organising for solidarity back to people's homes. Once again, people can go to their neighbour's home or a local pub or cafe for a meeting. It also differs from labour organising in being rooted in the realm of social reproduction and hence often led by women. 'Social reproduction' may seem like a jargon feminist term, but it refers to something very real: the work needed to create the homes in which people are born, formed and sustained. 'Home is an intimate space,' as one CHTU organiser pointed out to me, 'We might have to organise differently there to a workplace.' As tenant organisers we can also think of social reproduction as not just referring to individual homes, but to the communal realities and new possibilities for shared caring among those who live close to each other. In the potent mix of organising and proximity of living, there is potential for all kinds of new solidarities to emerge. The structure of people's lives, deliberately fragmented by neoliberalism, can begin to be reassembled. Tenant unions are building towards what people need politically: new forms of collective power, undergirded by the democratic and egalitarian belief that people deserve to be in control of their own housing, and of their own lives. What people also need, as LATU have realised, is to reconstruct or build upon geographically close communities that can become networks of support and mutual aid in the face of material and political adversity. This is slow work, but on some level it is the most important work: to remind people that they matter to each other, that they can support each other, that they need not live their life alone, that a life of solidarity awaits if they only reach out and grasp it.

4

Building Power from the Grassroots

It is a Wednesday evening in a community hall in London. Outside it is dark and cold but inside a warm buzz of conversation fills the air as a London Renters Union branch meeting gets going. A member calls for the meeting to start and the noise dies down as people take their seats. Just as that is happening, a man arrives late and takes a seat, looking disgruntled. The meeting opens with discussion of a local election campaign but he does not participate in the break-out groups or makes only gruff comments as though impatient with the process. We break for some dinner, cooked by one of the members. As we eat, I overhear him complaining about the union 'letting him down'. He had come to a previous meeting and the outcome had not been as he had hoped. It seems he had understood the union to be a service provider and he feels he has not had the service expected. My heart sinks, because once someone gets into this mentality it is usually difficult to get them out of it, despite all our explanations that we are not a service provision union.

This loudly voiced complaint aside, the meal is a time of easy sociality, and the mood in the room is buoyant as we form small groups for 'peer support' sessions. This is the part of the meeting where the union precisely doesn't perform a service, in the sense of offering to solve people's problems for them. Rather, it encourages an exchange of knowledge and skills in order to help people address their housing problems together. I sit in the same group as the man who came late, and he opens with his story of what the union has done wrong. What happens next is almost magical. As he talks about his housing disrepair problems, others in the group explain that they've had the same problems. Some of them had resolved it successfully by doing what he had been advised to do at the last meeting. Since that hadn't worked, they had other suggestions for him. Over the course of just a few minutes the man lost all his hostility. He saw that others were in the same boat as him. They didn't owe him anything, they were simply willing to share their experiences and knowledge in an act of mutual aid, and that was enough to open up new paths for him to resolve his situation. This is the experience of commonality that can be built through tenant union members supporting each other with their problems. Typically, members talk about the hope they find in understanding that they are not alone. From the community experience of meeting together, and from commonality of experience, springs solidarity. From that growing trust, victories small and large can be won. The experienced members are a necessary part of this kind of housing mutual aid, for what is needed beyond commonality is an understanding of what can be done to solve a personal housing crisis. The long-standing members will remember what has been tried with similar cases in the past, what has worked, what has not. They'll also know enough to let people down gently with problems the union can't solve – conflict between housemates or roommates being a prime one, for without a clear enemy, such as a landlord, there is no way to clearly judge rights and wrongs or to understand the landscape of power. What most new members will experience, however, is someone saying, 'Oh yes, we've dealt with a case like this before. What worked was this.' Nothing is more useful for building the confidence of the new member than to learn that they were right to be upset, and that disputes like theirs have been won before.

To understand the value of the confidence that joining a tenant union brings, it is important to be aware of the ways in which the housing system will undermine tenants' confidence. Renters who complain about mould in their home will often face their landlord coming in to paint over the mould, failing utterly to address the causes. If they complain to the local authority, as they are meant to in the UK, their absolute certainty that the mould problem hasn't been addressed will be undermined by a weak system of enforcement against landlords. Council officers will receive the photo of a newly painted wall from the landlord and respond saying that they are happy it has been dealt with. Do they really believe this, or are they just responding to the pressures of their job, underfunded and understaffed? From the outside it's hard to know, but the effect on tenants is the same: representatives of officialdom, who have the only official power to compel their landlord to act, deny the reality that they know to be true. For some people in good mental health, this may be merely infuriating, for those in poor mental health already, this type of assault on common sense can have serious effects. Why not give in to depression or paranoia when officialdom denies reality to your face? A few weeks later, the mould reappears. The disempowered tenant may or may not have the energy to start all over again.

Then there is the contempt with which tenants are treated. One LRU member, Kirsty, experienced this live during a television interview one day when the presenter sidetracked a discussion of the problem of no-fault evictions by claiming that some tenants didn't even know how to change a lightbulb and weren't even 'qualified' to be tenants. Kirsty slapped the presenter down for her patronising attitude, trying to steer the interview back on track. On the face of it this was a puzzling rant for a high-profile professional presenter to indulge in, but by her own admission she was a landlord herself. The agents of landlords naturally also share the contemptuous attitudes of landlords towards tenants. When I looked around a property in London, hunting for a house to buy for a housing co-operative, the agent wrongly assumed that I was looking for a family house. He proceeded to explain all the improvements an owner would want to make if they were moving their family in here. 'But it's not worth doing all that if you're going to rent it out,' he hastily added. 'This is fine as it is for a rental property.' The shoddy finishes, bodged repairs and poor communal space were good enough for mere tenants.

Unfortunately, some of the worst contempt directed at tenants comes from those tasked with caring for them as a public service. In the UK, council officers in the housing department and property managers for housing associations repeatedly let tenants know, either explicitly or implicitly, that they aren't worth taking any trouble over. The messaging is constant: maintenance reporting systems that seem to send complaints into the void, denial that a tenant has called about a problem at all (always put it in writing, we have to say), emergency numbers that don't get answers while a tenant's apartment has no water. Over and over again, the tenants have to learn that they don't matter to the people who have power over them.

Social media housing influencer Kwajo Tweneboa, based in London, has brought some of the worst offences of social landlords to light. He makes short, impactful videos showing flats covered in mould, or water pouring from ceilings, and calls out the land-lords who have refused to act. Such is his social media presence that most of those particular problems get sorted out quickly, but any number of situations just as bad continue around the country on a daily basis. In one temporary accommodation block we were organising, a pipe had broken in an empty flat, causing a small river of water to flow under the front door and down the corridor. Desperate calls to the council, to the landlord, to council building inspectors, found very few people interested or willing to take a call on a Saturday. Eventually, the landlord's agents promised to send someone to fix it on Monday. 'So you're going to leave this river of water flowing down the corridor to other flats for two days?' asked a tenant in disbelief. 'What if your own family lived here? Would you be happy with that?' But empathy doesn't pay well, so the agent wouldn't be drawn into answering, and the council that had placed tenants in the building went quiet. Eventually, the fire brigade had to break into the flat and stop the water, which hardly seemed a good use of public resources – but at least someone considered this crisis affecting mere tenants to be worth attending to.

This contempt by administrators of publicly managed housing is demonstrated by actions but it is also spoken. 'I deserve better than this,' claims a tenant whose heating doesn't work in midwinter. 'Why?' the council housing officer demands to know. There is no answer that can be given to this type of aggression if the officer doesn't agree that all humans deserve good housing. Temporary accommodation tenants are frequently told, usually while complaining about poor housing, that they are lucky to have anything at all. They could be on the street, they are reminded. Unfortunately, the logic of neoliberalism and austerity, which demands under-re-sourcing of every public service, means that the best housing officers leave the job, frustrated that they can't do it properly. Many of those who stay are those who are hardened to the complaints of their tenants. 'You don't want to be sent to live an hour and a half from your child's school?' said one to a member of LRU. 'We're sending some people three hours away. You're lucky they can stay at their school at all.' If a tenant doesn't have ironclad confidence, it's easy to get ground down by the thousand insults, big and small, that the housing system throws their way.

When Leila (not her real name) encountered LRU she had been in a terrible housing situation for a long time. She had been complaining for years about persistent disrepair and pest infestations in her flat, for which her housing association landlord would blame her. After meeting LRU on the street, she got herself to a branch meeting, by which point she had been temporarily moved out of her flat to a hotel. She told me about her experience afterwards:

> It felt like a lot of new people to meet at once. The meeting was quite packed. We broke out into groups and when it came to me – it was difficult to tell, tell them about rats and mice and how the house nearly burned down, about not having any water. But when I started I couldn't stop. When I came back in the room mentally, everyone's mouths were open in shock … You're made to feel for so long that it's your fault, and you don't have the network. You start to wonder, is it my fault? … But I got back to the hotel that evening and started thinking 'That was really empowering.'

What followed was a classic union campaign of collective approaches to her landlord, followed by public media shaming and a small protest. Leila won what she needed – a new flat with a permanent contract. She said, 'I don't believe I would ever have won my case if I had not had LRU. Collective action spurred me on. Working with other people with housing problems also spurred me on.' The collectivity referred to here was the organising within her LRU branch, while in other cities it might primarily be building-based. Solidarity not only wins cases, it also restores people to their sense of being significant, in the midst of a system that tries to make them insignificant. It creates a feeling of power in collectivity that is never forgotten, often bringing self-respect and confidence back with it. Landlords developed their contempt for tenants through having too much power. The tenant union's answer to their contempt is to build power stronger than theirs and defeat them.

The power inherent in the position of landlord seems to make landlords around the world see their tenants as less than fully human. Catherine Porter, a researcher with Syracuse Tenant Union in the state of New York, explained some experiences of union members:

> Tenant interviewees lament the lack of empathy by landlords, whose negligence has real, devastating impacts on families. After Darlene learned her children had lead poisoning, 'never once did this man [her landlord] ever come knock on my door and say, "Hey, you know what? I apologize. I didn't know it was there. Let's work together to try to remediate –" or whatever. I got none of that. Instead, I got him driving up behind me acting like he was gonna run me over,' referring to an incident when Darlene talked to a reporter about her experience and her landlord immediately threatened her. Barbara finds that out-of-town landlords don't care about property conditions, but 'expect rent every month and then if you call them about certain things, they either don't come or, you know, they … just don't fix it. When they send someone to fix it, instead of fixing it the right way by code, they are putting a Band-Aid over it.'[1]

What this widespread, internationalised, largely unchallenged contempt by landlords says is that the position of the landlord is a class position. Their class position poisons the ability of many landlords to empathise, while the unaccountable power says that they don't have to. Any time unaccountable power of one section of a population over another becomes commonplace, so too does abuse of that power. Since they are able to abuse their power, the landlord then has to justify what they do in their own minds, and this has the usual dynamics: racialised, gendered and prejudiced against those born less fortunate than themselves. The landlord doesn't think of themselves as a bad person, but neither do they think of their tenant as their equal. In their heads, consciously or unconsciously, they are likely to frame the tenant as 'a gangbanger', a 'slutty single mother' or, where no other handle can be found, simply as a 'loser' who has failed to live up to their potential under capitalism.

LEARNING THE LANDSCAPE

Empowering the individual tenant against their landlord is the start of building power. As London Renters Union matured, it moved from throwing everything at each housing case, to being more selective about which cases to put more energy into. It has discovered with experience that a lot of cases can be solved by a letter to an estate agent, or a claim to a deposit holding company. These small actions can be taken on by the members themselves, and organisers encourage members to do what they can for themselves, armed with a little more knowledge from talking to others. Rather than this being about leaving members to struggle, the idea is to empower the members to take control of their own housing issues so that they can move forward with an improved understanding of their rights and with new-found skills. This follows a standard community organising principle of not doing anything for people that they can do for themselves. Community organisers have always known that an action is not empowering if it treats people as dependents. The principle of getting people to lead their own cases has dual benefits, for the union as a whole can now put more energy into cases that will clearly need collective action to solve them, which will require a process of building solidarity in order to win victory. It is also about building that confidence up in individuals as they learn to organise and learn how to build power.

Within this process the tenant becomes an organised and organising tenant, and so begins to do things they couldn't have dreamt of alone. 'I never imagined I could be in a room with the mayor [of the borough] telling them my experience,' one low-income LRU member told me after a local electoral campaign. 'We asked for the council to do things and they said yes. LRU has made this possible.' Empowering the individual tenant is important, but it must lead to the next step: empowering collectivities, and projecting collective power into or against political institutions.

A housing group in Berlin mentioned above, Stop Evictions, decided to build solidarity in the community through organising around a single tactic. They do what their name says: their tactic is to gather at the site of any eviction they know of and physically block the eviction from occurring. They aren't a tenant union but rather a group of people who choose to use this particular method. They do share many of the goals of a tenant union. One activist told me, 'We live in capitalism, there is a lot of exploitation and oppression. We see evictions as kind of a spike that represents the whole structure. We see this detailed work of stopping every eviction as creating the basis for overcoming capitalism. The goal is zero evictions, but to do that we have to win much else.' As with most tenant unions, there is long-term thinking here among the short-term battles. The atomisation of society must be broken down if we are to win anything worthwhile in the struggle against the economic forces that determine our lives. Tenant unions know that collective action wins results, it is the role of the union to find the situations in which it can be most effective, then leverage that into bigger victories.

It is important for tenant unions not to assume they know exactly how to organise from the start. The community organising must emerge from what the community needs, and power is built upon addressing those needs. As LRU learnt about the housing land-scape, we discovered more about a category of housing that most people in the UK don't give much thought to: temporary accom-modation. LRU was not the first to organise in this sector: one inspiring group called Focus E15 in East London had hit the head-lines some years previously with a campaign against their hostel being closed down. But learning how common and everyday the policy of placing people in 'temporary accommodation' had become was a surprise to many in LRU who were new to housing organising.

Tenants in temporary accommodation are on the list for a council house, lists that run to hundreds of thousands of families across the UK. Even within a town or borough, a tenant might easily be the thousandth on the list for a house. Those on the list who have the resources are left to stew alone in the private rented sector, but those with additional vulnerabilities or particularly on low income may qualify for temporary accommodation. Due to the racialised nature of class in the UK, many of these tenants in London are people of colour, often recent migrants with citizenship, refugee status or indefinite leave to remain. In some London boroughs, 10 per cent of children are stuck in temporary accommodation. That amounts to many tens of thousands of children whose lives are blighted by precarious housing. Some of them will not escape even when they become adults. I met one man who had been a temporary accommodation tenant for ten years.

At its worst, this state of housing limbo can mean being housed in a hostel with strangers for months at a time. At its best, it can mean a decent flat to live in while the tenant (and usually their family, since most people in temporary accommodation have families) wait for a permanent home. A lot of temporary accommodation residents are somewhere in between these poles, and many of them end up in the semi-permanent purgatory of blocks of flats owned by private landlords but where the council acts as an intermediary, renting the whole block – or different councils renting different parts of a block, as we discovered in one of LRU's more challenging organising efforts.

These blocks of 'temporary' homes tend to be low quality and poorly maintained, because if they weren't the landlords could get more money renting them individually. The responsibility for maintenance is usually with the private landlord, but since the individual in the block has no choice about being there, the landlord feels little real pressure to do the maintenance. It is the council that moves tenants into these blocks and usually the council that moves them out: temporary accommodation residents can be moved around at the council's whim, getting kicked off the waiting list for a permanent home if they refuse new temporary accommodation. As a result, they are often forced to live with intermittent water, sparking electrics, mouldy walls that give children asthma or unsealed windows. If they complain, they are often told by council officers to be grateful for a roof over their heads. Technically they are still tenants, but as happens in other countries such as the US, when people are placed in private accommodation by local authorities they end up in the position of service users with no rights, rather than having the rights of tenants. The landlords revel in it.

Some of these blocks were converted from offices under a controversial UK planning right that allows conversion from office to residential use without planning permission. These buildings were never built to be homes and they never should have become homes. The councils say they can't afford anything else, and it's better than people being on the street. The central government doesn't care; they are a government for the winners and these people are not winning. The landlords, naturally, are winning. While they can't ever charge premium rents for their shoddy properties, they can get more from the council than they would get on the market. It is one of the biggest rackets in the UK, and the outcome of all this is that many of the worst slumlords in the UK are funded by taxes. It should be a scandal, but short of the occasional story in liberal outlets like the *Guardian*, it is a non-story, a story about people who don't matter, in places nobody cares about. The lives of people living precariously, made unnecessarily even more precarious and more miserable, are not news.

However, accidentally, and entirely unconsciously, the councils have put tenants in a good position for organising. For each such block of temporary accommodation there are two pressure points: the single landlord, and the council that doesn't want to be shown to be housing people in slum accommodation. Every large city and some smaller towns in the UK have blocks like this now, but they don't announce themselves. There are no signs up saying they are housing temporary accommodation residents. Plenty of people walk by without even knowing that temporary accommodation exists. To know about these buildings, it is vital to be organising in the local community. And so it is that LRU has won hundreds of thousands of pounds in repairs for temporary accommodation residents over the years, and helped many residents move into better housing. One tenant told a meeting of the union, 'London Renters Union saved my life, really. I will be forever so grateful that they made the council move me. They just ignored me! But with the union I am strong.' There have been impressive collective victories too, with building roofs repaired and new bathrooms and kitchens installed in one block after tenants in the union organised protests at their situation.

There is a lesson here that can be generalised beyond London or the UK. Temporary accommodation is a particular dysfunction arising from the historical obligation on local authorities in the UK to house everybody who needs it, in conjunction with a free market/austerity project that prevents them building decent homes to put people in. But across the Global North, poverty and desperation in housing hides in plain sight. People often barely know their neighbours, let alone the living situation in the block down the road. To understand the organising opportunities locally, a tenant union has to either be composed of people already embedded in the community – and in our atomised societies fewer such people exist than used to be the case – or they need to get boots on the ground: knocking on doors, stopping people in the streets, asking questions. If they want to even understand the housing problems in their locality, let alone address them, tenant unions have no choice but to get to know their local communities, to make themselves part of the local landscape so that people know where to turn when they have problems. Only then does the atomised desperation in housing come to light. Only then do tenant unions have the chance to turn atomisation into new community, and desperation into camaraderie and solidarity.

GROWING THE BASE

The building of solidarity and power around both single housing disputes and larger building disputes where people are having shared experiences is a key part of what it means to most unions to be building power from the base. Even if the union is an institution with a legal constitution (not all of them are), in reality it is built upon a foundation of mutual aid and community solidarity. This may sound like sloganeering, but it means practical things. It means that if a landlord is trying to illegally evict a member, they will find their way literally blocked by a small crowd of union members. It means that if an estate agent is trying to steal a deposit, they will find their office shut down by protests until they concede. It means that if a social landlord won't do repairs, their reputation will be dragged through the mud by a concerted social media campaign. It means that if people in a building are suffering the same housing problems, they will be brought together to make them stronger. Each time a small victory is won, the union has flexed its muscles and built power, become even stronger for the next fight.

In the UK, housing casework in the private sector is more often about confronting landlords or agents of individual properties, but in much of Europe and North America, the basic organising happens around large buildings owned by one landlord. For Crown Heights Tenant Union this is the bread and butter of their work. They will picket a landlord's office, even their homes, and publicly shame the landlords however they can. In the face of divide-and-rule tactics by landlords, the union's aim is often a collective bargaining agreement. The landlord must sit at the table with everyone, and the principle is laid down that everyone in the building should be treated the same and should be treated well. Those on controlled rents should get their repairs done. Those middle-class incomers being overcharged should have their rents returned to controlled levels.

Key skills for North American tenant unions, then, involve learning to create building committees or associations among residents of a single building. Within this building organising, a rent strike is the ultimate weapon. In New York, the rent strike truly came to the fore during the COVID-19 pandemic. A CHTU organiser told me how the idea seemed to spread like wildfire. In building after building, those who had been organised with CHTU reported they were on rent strike. Within a couple of months, up to 40 per cent of New York tenants were no longer paying rent, though the degree to which they were formally organised in their buildings differed significantly. Those already organised with CHTU had a much greater chance of constructing true solidarity in the face of landlord demands, and some of the buildings' tenants remained on rent strike for months longer than in unorganised buildings, with tenants in one CHTU building even staying on strike for years. New tenant organisations were also popping up. Brooklyn Eviction Defense Tenant Union came into being during the pandemic and is still going strong, organising rent strikes around issues such as building neglect and safety now that the pandemic lockdown moment has passed.

Los Angeles Tenants Union sees building organising as a way to build power too, but for them it is about moving beyond housing justice. It is a method for building solidarity, of course, but it must consist of active solidarity led by the tenants. 'We ask people if they want to fight for themselves,' an organiser told me. 'And we tell them outright that if they don't fight for themselves then no-one will. It's not our job in the union to fight on people's behalf.' The union is there to help people come together, but the members must accept the nature of their situation: that alone they have too little power, and the only way to win power is through collective struggle.

Typically for LATU, the union sees building organising as having a pedagogical function. One of the aims is to create among members a 'new common sense'. This learning happens more through action than through overt teaching. Organisers told me that tenants in a building organising themselves collectively might give notice to the landlord, say of 15 days, to make repairs or refuse to pay the rent. Their members are sometimes disappointed when the repairs are done because they wanted the confrontation. Through taking action they have realised that they have power in numbers, that if one of them doesn't pay the rent it is their problem, but if all of them don't pay the rent it is the landlord's problem. Communities fighting together, LATU organisers say, can have a transformative effect on how individuals view the world and the action that it's possible for them to take.

When tenant unions talk of organising communities, the term 'community' often means aiming wider than the block. Most tenant unions explicitly position themselves against gentrification and that can draw them into wider fights, sometimes under the banner of a wider 'right to the city'. Like Greater Manchester Tenant Union fighting to save a local pub, this requires them to defend more than simply residential property. London Renters Union has found itself fighting for stallholders in Ridley Road Market in rapidly gentrifying Dalston. Berlin housing campaigners have inevitably found themselves defending the city's once-vibrant but now disappearing anarchist social centres.

How much time this wider organising occupies varies from union to union and over time. A CATU organiser told me they spend around 10 per cent of their time defending 'community amenities', and this seems a likely figure for other UK unions too. But at particular moments a union or a branch or chapter of a union may put significant energy into fighting for a particular community amenity. The unions are engaged in wider anti-gentrification fights because they feel a political imperative to fight for the wider community, but the realities of housing struggle mean most tenant unions have little time to spare beyond their basic work, so these peaks of non-housing activity will rarely last long.

Moving beyond housing campaigning is nonetheless important, for it is a great way for a union to get to know their wider community and to meet people that organisers might otherwise have little contact with. In London at least, many markets are staffed largely by recent immigrants, so building solidarity with market traders is potentially a doorway to discovering entire communities hidden in the area. The same is true of churches, community centres, playgrounds, laundromats, twelve-step meetings and other community commons. What small fragments of community still exist in an atomised city can be found around these amenities, so building power in the community requires a vision that sees somewhat beyond housing.

TAKING ON THE ASSET MANAGERS

Organising for tenant power requires both a near focus in the community and a far focus, looking well beyond the community. It is an important feature of the current tenant organising landscape that there are far bigger targets than local landlords or local authorities. The last couple of decades have seen the rise and rise of the asset management industry. This branch of the financial sector moved into residential property in a big way after the financial crisis, as laid out by Brett Christophers in his book *Our Lives in Their Portfolios: Why Asset Managers Own the World.*[2] He explains how asset managers such as BlackRock, Blackstone and Vanguard have bought into property as they have understood how to make it more lucrative. They are looking for the returns not only from current rents, and not only from property price inflation, but from the uplift in property value they can get by turning the screws on tenants to lift rents to the maximum. This means that a big asset manager taking over your building is almost certainly bad news.

The process of asset managers colonising the property market is more advanced in some countries than others. In the UK, it is still in its infancy, in part because buying individual properties requires more management than buying whole blocks of flats; while in Spain, what campaigners called 'vulture funds' swooped in after their financial crisis, scooping up thousands of properties while prices were at a historical low. The US, unsurprisingly, has significant numbers of domestic rental properties under the management of large investment funds. The global reach of the giant asset managers is both a threat and an opportunity. Once a fund is rich enough to be invested on every continent, they have the power to buy politicians and distort local politics. But being everywhere means that they can be targeted everywhere. Sindicat de Llogaters spotted exactly this when they wanted to fight back against Blackstone in Barcelona. Alongside Madrid tenant union campaigners, they issued an invitation to housing campaign organisations worldwide to join a social media storm against Blackstone's presence in their city. I will quote the appeal that arrived in my inbox at length, since I can't do any better than their communications team in explaining the action:

> Blackstone is the biggest real estate investor in Spain, a vulture fund from the United States whose business model focuses on speculating with people's homes. Their portfolio includes not only 20,000 homes but also a big number of hotels, including this one. They play a key role in increasing the touristification and gentrification of our cities, as well as the unbearable rent increases we are currently facing. In the last 10 years, Blackstone has evicted more than 1 million families in Spain, by pressuring them into moving out after increasing their rent massively. Enough is enough!
>
> Join us today in shaming Blackstone for kicking us out of our neighbourhoods and our cities. No more impunity! Our lives are not market goods – we deserve to live in decent homes. We demand all evictions be stopped. We demand Blackstone offer fair rents to all those families who have built a home for years

and now have to flee due to the abuse and harassment they have suffered ...

Blackstone has a global presence – our movement for fair housing also does! That's why we are here today, both in Barcelona and Madrid, fighting for our rights against a common enemy at the same time. Don't let them play with our lives, it could be you and your loved ones soon! Join us in the struggle against real estate speculation.

ACTION! The Tenants Unions of Madrid and Barcelona are occupying hotels owned by @blackstone to demand that it respect the right to housing. STOP evictions, ENOUGH speculation!

ATTENTION! The vulture fund @blackstone is not only the largest owner of residential property in Spain but also of hotels. Today, fellow activists and members of the Tenants Unions in Madrid and Barcelona have paid a visit to their hotels demanding an end to evictions.

The appeal went out across Europe, it went out across the Atlantic to the US and, buoyed up by an agitprop song written against Blackstone, the tenant unions proceeded to shame the fund on an international stage. Families directly affected by Blackstone joined the occupation of the hotels, chanting *nos quedamos, nos quedamos* – we are staying – protesting unaffordable rent rises designed to push them out of their homes. This claim is not just posturing, for tenant unions are winning successes. Madrid's tenant union, Sindicato de Inquilinos e Inquilinas, has forced Blackstone to the negotiating table and won stable rents for hundreds of members.

As asset managers take over more and more housing, it becomes ever-more necessary to build power against them. We know that they buy buildings with the intention of raising rents. Studies in the US have shown that asset manager owners of residential properties evict their tenants more frequently than other landlords. The stakes are too high to leave the asset managers unchallenged. As international solidarity between tenant unions solidifies in the coming years, the tactic of coordinated international rent strikes against asset managers becomes a real possibility. This is not an easy tactic to develop and it may take some time to win successes. Can solidarity really hold together across oceans when landlords try to buy out one set of strikers? Do asset managers sit on such large cash reserves and income streams that the strike would have to be unfeasibly long to dent their profits? The only way to answer these questions will be to build international solidarity and launch the strikes, and so carve out a new future for tenant union action.

TACTICS FOR BUILDING POWER

The new tenant unions know that they cannot build their power over the long term simply by fighting on members' immediate housing issues. Mutual aid, union organisers are usually quick to point out, can only get so far in addressing housing crises. It's good to stop an illegal eviction happening, but how does a tenant union create a situation where no landlord would dare consider an illegal eviction? That means building power that goes beyond the neighbourhood and beyond even confronting landlords. In the medium term (I will address the long term in later chapters), the solidarity that is built around keeping members in houses in good repair will often be turned into wider solidarity through campaigning. This is not to say that all tenant unions get involved in campaigning, and I will discuss other strategic choices below, but most tenant unions keep half an eye on opportunities to change national or local laws.

In the UK, this might be a local campaign like forcing the local council to do more repairs on its housing stock. In other countries with more local powers, it might be about localised rent control. Many tenant unions are also engaged in national campaigns, aimed at, say, making tenancies indefinite or establishing national rent control, often through coalitions. Whether the campaigning is aimed at the local level or nationally, unions often face a choice about how they balance the energy they put into fighting individual or block housing disputes versus the energy that goes into their campaigning. This is not an easy balance to strike. One LRU organiser admitted to me that if there was a way to build solidarity for campaigning without the housing casework, he might just do that. The housing disputes inevitably take up a huge amount of energy. Some days it can feel like a distraction from fixing the systemic issues (in the regulatory regime, that is – there are broader ideas of what the systemic issues might be that I will discuss later).

Why spend time getting one landlord to comply with the law when the union could be campaigning to set up an enforcement system against landlords that would make them live in fear of doing anything illegal? Why try to get one person bumped up the social housing list when the union could be campaigning to build half a million more social rented homes? Yet it is the casework that builds solidarity and draws in new members. A union that didn't do the housing casework would barely be a union.

Trade unions face the same dilemmas about how to spend their energy in workplace struggles. How much time do they want to spend winning back stolen pay packets, and how much time do they want to spend campaigning to make wage theft a commonly prosecuted criminal offence? They know that if they can achieve the latter, then wage theft would shrink to a tenth of what it is today, but they can't know if that battle is winnable, and in the meantime, members need support today. Of course, over the long term trade unions have done plenty of both, but that is over the very long term, with high membership densities at times and with plenty of resources to mobilise. New tenant unions are starting from scratch, as small and weak as trade unions were when they first started out. That is not to downplay the victories of previous generations of tenant unions, which in some places won many victories, ranging from indefinite tenancies to rent control. But the conditions have been such under neoliberalism, and through the boom in home-buying, that the political energy went out of those unions.[3] The new tenant unions find themselves having to build up a movement that has not been a movement for a long time. It is necessarily slow work to mobilise sufficient resources to target national-level institutions.

While the new tenant unions are usually clear that they engage in mutual aid and therefore they are organisations of *tenants*, when it comes to campaigning there are advantages to bringing on board members who aren't tenants. Homeowners with more comfortable lives may well have more energy to spare to offer to a long-term campaign. The Berlin DWE campaign made no distinction between tenants and homeowners precisely because it was a campaign and was happy to take the time of anyone who offered it. But as mentioned earlier, Living Rent in Scotland, having started as purely a tenant union, have also seen advantages in expanding their membership criteria to include homeowners. Catalonia's Sindicat and LRU also allow homeowners to join. This may sometimes be about taking on the struggles of low-income homeowners, as Living Rent was keen to do. But it also recognises that broader campaigns benefit from having as many people involved as possible, including some more privileged people who are willing to expend their privilege on the daily grind of campaigning.

Both campaigning and housing disputes can be exciting to work on, offering beautiful moments of solidarity, but both can carry risks for tenant unions. The campaigning carries a risk – quite high in countries where neoliberalism is strongest – that the union will fail to win significant victories. Every campaigning organisation of the left must face that possibility, but not all of them have to contend with the strength of the forces arrayed against housing reform. If we are being honest, we must admit that much campaigning on housing has failed to make a mark in recent years. In the UK, housing victories have been very thin on the ground, often due to weak social movements, but also due to the hegemonic position of the homeowner bloc. Even in California, where huge campaigns in favour of rent control can be mobilised, based in cities with much historical and current housing organising – notably Los Angeles, San Francisco and Oakland – victory is not assured. Californian campaigners have had to face the huge setback of the Costa-Hawkins Act, a state-wide Act limiting rent control. The fightback against that Act continues, but it demonstrates how demoralising campaigning can be when it doesn't pay off. These difficulties hint at the deeper systemic problems that block opportunities for better housing for ordinary people. That systemic landscape is also the reason why some tenant unions barely do campaigning at all: rather than seeing themselves as facing a problematic regulatory or development regime, they want to address the deeper issues of capitalism, to which mainstream politicians turn a distinctly deaf ear.

The housing dispute casework offers a lower risk of failure – in the UK at least, tenant unions win many more cases than they lose – but the energy-consuming nature of it carries a risk of burnout. 'It's a lot of work and it's exhausting,' one organiser for Living Rent told me frankly. The organisation encourages members heavily involved in running their 'member defence' meetings and cases to take breaks. What most tenant unions discover is that it is hard for people to cope with other people's housing troubles on their minds all the time. Living Rent provides training to those members who run the member defence meetings in how to do it, giving them the title of 'member defence officer'. This means there is a cost in time and resources if the trained members then burn out and drop out of doing the work altogether. Thus, the training must include teaching people how to look after themselves and step back when they are getting exhausted. While Living Rent has some paid staff, they don't take the lead on member defence. Their key role is specifically to do organising, as in London Renters Union. Living Rent, moving in the direction of its partner organisation ACORN, now calls itself a 'tenant and community union', opening itself up to campaigning on more than just housing. But it still focuses mostly on housing cases, and it is unpaid members who must bear the burden of this vital aspect of building power.

The energy and time it takes to fight housing disputes should not be underestimated. As one Barcelona organiser admitted to me, 'Being part of the Sindicat is difficult if you don't have a lot of time. Even those who want to commit, but who have partners who aren't involved, find it difficult to participate as much as they want to.' This creates something of a contradiction: organisers always want to make the union more accessible and diverse, but the nature of fighting housing battles makes it difficult to know how to reduce the workload for those involved. Even among young, white, university-educated tenants, something as ordinary as having a child can make it almost impossible to participate. For migrants living precarious lives, on low income and with multiple caring responsibilities, it's a tall order to ask them to commit to fighting other people's housing disputes. It is for this practical reason, as well as the wider desire for systemic change, that most tenant unions want to win campaigns that will reduce the need for individual or building-level housing disputes.

Tenant unions face a constant balancing act then: fighting for broader housing rights and tackling individual tenant problems are both crucial. To manage this workload and ensure member well-being, some unions get creative. Greater Manchester Tenant

Union has come up with an unusual – at least in Europe – way to help support overstretched union members. Those members who are elected to the committee who do more than 20 hours work in a month for the union can receive a payment of up to £200. This allows low-income members, perhaps those in precarious zero-hour contracts, to dedicate time to the union without sacrificing paid work. Even a small payment can significantly reduce stress and free up time. The experiment is in its early days, but it seems plausible that it will be good for diversity on the GMTU committee, allowing more precarious members to join and commit their time. Other unions focus on empowering members to help each other. The Bond Precaire Woonvormen in the Netherlands connects tenants under the same landlord via WhatsApp groups. This fosters new mutual aid and reduces the burden on experienced members who might otherwise be constantly needed for support. While these methods don't eliminate the need for broader union solidarity, increasing member involvement in mutual aid expands the overall capacity of the tenant union.

Talk of such challenges while trying to make a case in favour of tenant unions may seem unnecessarily negative. But the argument for tenant unions is not that they are always easy to build, it is that they are an exciting and necessary form for our times. As tricky as it might be for tenant unions to juggle the competing pressures and risks of campaigning and housing casework, we know that they are doing it, and that they are growing in numbers and in power. Tens of thousands of people are involved in this work because, despite the challenges, the rewards of tenant union organising are immense. Members join a community, and ever afterwards know that they need never be alone in facing their landlord. Their vulnerability in the housing system can be converted into collective power. Tenant unions hold out hope to people who thought they had been left to fend for themselves. They build solidarity and a new power base in communities riven by division and capitalist ideology. While many of the new tenant unions are still young, they have already established themselves as institutions of the left that will last for decades, even generations. Tenant unions are changing the landscape of organising and, as they build power, will change the landscape of housing too.

5

Different Strategies, United Tenants

For 10 years and counting, long-term and new tenants in the Crown Heights Tenant Union [CHTU] have united to fight landlords and the landlord system ...

We will fight until we have justice and an end to rent fraud, over-charge, and the landlord system that enables it. CHTU demands universal rent control; that all 'deregulated' apartments must be automatically and immediately restored to rent-stabilization and rents must be rolled back to the last true rent registration, as has been the law since 2019. The State must do this pre-emptively and immediately. We demand reparations to all displaced tenants, and we demand that illegally overcharged tenants are paid the full triple penalty on their overcharges. Landlords who have illegally destabilized units must lose ownership of buildings. We refuse to allow the landlord class to continue to attack tenants and enrich themselves with the State's blessing. The Crown Heights Tenant Union and the tenant movement – one part of the broader workers' movement everywhere – will fight for and win a better world after the landlord system. (Statement by Crown Heights Tenant Union, 21 December 2022)

Block by block to a world without rent. (Theme of Los Angeles Tenant Union's 2022 Annual Assembly)

I am sitting outside a bar having a beer on one of the many cross-roads of Barcelona's famous urban grid, chatting with housing organisers from around Europe. The night is warm and, while this isn't part of the city's famous large-scale pedestrianisation experiment, the traffic is quiet and rarely disturbs our conversation. We are all attending a conference of housing movement organisations being hosted by the Sindicat de Llogaters. I explain to a member of the Sindicat that the activities of LRU are rarely focused on political parties or getting friendly with politicians. We do some lobbying, I add, but largely we have to view government and political parties as opponents we must push into adopting positions they would rather not take.

The situation here in Barcelona, the Sindicat organiser tells me over the babble of voices around us, is quite different. A couple of years previously Ada Colau, a founder member of the PAH, had become mayor of Barcelona, buoyed by a wave of left-wing party organising that happened in the wake of Spain's 15-M or *Indignados* movement. Organisers in the Sindicat now personally know people who work for the municipal government. That doesn't mean getting the city to do the right thing is easy, for there are many counterforces against change, but it does make the possibility of genuine influence seem very real.

We leave the bar to go to a party in a squat run by political activists on the edge of town. There is an unwalled tent structure with a sound system inside and a wood-fired hot-tub built by the residents. As the party gets going, the Sindicat member I had been chatting to earlier points out to me someone on the dance floor: 'They are now on the city council. I've always known them from places like this. This is the situation we're in now.'

Genuine power that can be wielded to change the housing landscape and put a permanent end to housing crises is unlikely to grow accidentally. Nor does it emerge spontaneously from a hundred acts of solidarity, or a campaign win here and there. To turn mutual aid and housing campaigning into real power requires a strategy. Even wins at city level, such as Kansas City Tenants' defeat of evictions during the pandemic, outlined below, requires a sharp strategy. To win good housing for millions of people surely requires an even more robust plan for how to get from 'housing crisis' to housing justice. Building a base of tenant power is all very well, but how and in what direction will that power be wielded? At least three factors are significant in determining the strategies that tenant unions choose: their housing environment, their political environment, and the political priorities and experiences of the key organisers, which often determine key goals. I shall discuss how each of these modulates the strategy of tenant unions, and even results in significant variation in strategy between unions. We can never think about tenant union strategy as being fixed. Organisers in most tenant unions explicitly say that within their young organisations strategies are still being formed. When LATU organisers spoke to me about their strategy, what they wanted to talk about was the new definition of their work that had emerged from their 2023 're-founding' event, which had resulted in the four goals explained in Chapter 2. Over time, the strategy in large organisations can become muddied, they felt, and some members had begun to see LATU as 'fighting for tenant rights', which might be a strategy that other tenant unions would aim for, but had never been the primary aim for LATU. In order to clarify who they were, LATU instituted a process with their base members that would allow those members to express their idea of struggle.

For unions making a concerted effort to challenge hierarchies and privileges, the 'key organisers' will necessarily be different people over time. The union strategy should ideally change with them, whether through ordinary democratic means or LATU's radical pedagogical approach. A strategy might also change with experience, as when LRU discovered that tenants in social housing needed the union's help. As a result, while I will discuss some strategies from different tenant unions in this chapter, and while I hope I will not misrepresent any of them, it's important to state that I can only present a snapshot image of union strategies.

Let's start this account of differing strategies by looking at recruitment strategies, where we will quickly see that the housing environment can make a significant difference to how unions approach their recruitment.

'A lot of people think they haven't had a bad time renting,' one LRU organiser told me. 'But then they join up and realise that they have a bad landlord. It happened to me. I had just normalised what was happening: being scared to ask to fix things in case it led to a rent rise, the house falling apart.' This demonstrates how the isolation of London living is increased by the structure of housing: most people live in a small home owned by one landlord, while their neighbours will either be owner-occupiers or tenants of another landlord. As renters, people are isolated, which means that, for LRU, overcoming the isolation is always a big part of the organising battle.

Paradoxically, the small landlord, while appearing less clearly 'evil' than a big landlord that is screwing tenants on behalf of investors, is often more difficult to fight. The common type of British housing – terraced or semi-detached – in which there are no shared corridors or lobbies with neighbours, means that many tenants never encounter their neighbours at all. Many LRU members have told me that they thought the problems they were having were unusual. Organisers are aware of this, and the need to combat the isolation. One organiser told me, 'Part of the experience of joining the union should be that people understand that loads of people in London are having similar experiences. There are common problems and so we have common interests.'

This is why it makes strategic sense for LRU to focus on the branch meeting as the locus of organising. It is a very social space, a nexus for overcoming isolation. The branch is a new community where none existed before, one that aims to reflect the diversity of London's renters. The desire to build relationships of trust within a diverse membership leads to LRU's recruitment strategy: that it builds slowly and carefully, trying to ensure that its branches reflect the areas they cover. For the union, this means intentionally ignoring the ease of recruitment through social media, since social media tends to attract young, mostly white members who are already politicised. It is the quickest way to attract attention, but it does not build a diverse community. Instead, the strategy for growth in LRU is to focus on the slow work of making connections one on one, meeting people on the streets or in community spaces.

As we have seen, CATU in Ireland underwent a rapid expansion during the pandemic, and this relied necessarily – given the lack of face-to-face interaction – on utilising social media to spread the word and recruit new members. This is also a result of the size of the territory across which CATU organises. Most tenant unions are built in one city, but CATU organises across a whole country and a disputed border. Perhaps for the same reason, Living Rent has not been shy of recruitment by social media, while city-based unions such as CHTU or LATU tend to prefer a focus on recruitment through organic links within communities.

These North American city-based tenant unions also construct themselves differently due to another factor: being built upon a base of tenant associations formed within particular buildings, where a single landlord is vulnerable to rent strikes in which significant income can be denied them. This means that the recruitment strategy will always be to locate buildings in which multiple tenants are having trouble, then maximising union density within that building, and the trainings of the unions tend to focus on this method of building. Organisers in New York can even find any other buildings their landlord owns with the help of the website 'Who Owns What'. The site is run by housing activists who understood that a landlord's 'diverse portfolio' can mean diverse opportunities to hit back at them. This building ownership structure, along with the shared spaces that are inherent to apartment living, helps make the building-based tenant association a powerful engine of tenant union recruitment in many densely developed cities. The Bay Area TANC unites residents with the same landlord in 'tenant councils', enabling those in different buildings to target their landlord together.

Here we can add something about union structure as a strategic issue. Within some unions, building organising seems to lead to a naturally more decentralised union structure, for much of the face-to-face meeting happens within buildings rather than centrally. In some US cities, this will naturally lead to some of the buildings being Spanish-speaking, while others will be English-speaking – and if the tenant union is making an effort to retain low-income members, like LATU, the central meetings will be held in both languages. However, it does not follow in a deterministic way that building organising will lead to a particular strategy or structure. In Barcelona, many tenants also live in large apartment buildings. In fact, Barcelona tenant organisers tend not to take on small, individual landlords for fear that public sympathies would be with the landlords – an option not available to organisers in the UK, where most tenants have a small landlord. So as a choice, most of the Sindicat's housing disputes occur in apartment buildings, but it is relatively rare for the Sindicat to put building organising front and centre of how it presents itself to the world. Rather, much of their public-facing work foregrounds the union's focus on a city-wide scale of organising and on pressuring formal institutions. This is at least partly the legacy of the success of the PAH in Spain, and the belief that a tenant union or network of tenant unions could become as influential as that organisation. Due to historical movement successes and the political leanings of their key organisers, the Sindicat is more drawn towards larger-scale fights, even as they build solidarity around building-level conflicts.

DANCES WITH GOVERNMENTS

This brings us neatly to strategy in relation to formal political institutions. Since Spain's *crisis*, the country has seen a lively revival of left-wing parties opposed to neoliberalism, as contrasted to the older left party PSOE which, like so many other centre-left parties across Europe, embraced the neoliberal consensus. These parties or alliances – Podemos, Barcelona en Comú, Sumar – have even achieved some level of power at both municipal and national levels. This has led to the political landscape with which I opened the chapter – that activists in tenant unions may personally know some of the people in power. This has not, sadly, led to an unconstrained ability to pass very left-wing policies, for the political climate still resists anything that breaks the neoliberal consensus. Ada Colau recently lost the mayorship of Barcelona, albeit to a socialist trade unionist who promised to make housing a priority. In her eight years in power, she has only been able to make small dents in Barcelona's ongoing housing crisis, and capital still rules in Barcelona. Even if the concrete achievements of these left parties are weaker than might be hoped, they do offer the hope to Spanish organisers that real change can be brought about through the electoral process.

Aside from the brief movements around Jeremy Corbyn in the UK and Bernie Sanders in the US, this path to change largely feels blocked in those countries, which continue to suffer in the grip of effective two-party systems in which both parties adhere to neoliberalism and colonialism at home and abroad. Unsurprisingly, Corbyn's left-wing Labour in opposition gave a sympathetic ear to tenant unions, but those days are now years in the past. Starmer's Labour, obsessed with appeasing the right-wing press and appearing non-threatening to those with power, presents only closed doors to campaigners demanding anything but the mildest tenancy reforms. It is natural enough, then, that the Sindicat de Llogaters and other Spanish tenant unions would be drawn towards a tactic of projecting themselves upwards into institutional political spaces, and equally natural that it would not be the first instinct of tenant unions in England or the US.

I deliberately referred to 'England' because Wales and Scotland have different political environments to Westminster. Scotland, with more autonomy than Wales, has a multi-party system of proportional representation, and this has created a more open door for Living Rent to campaign for national-level rent controls. They have not won everything they want, and to Scottish tenant campaigners it often feels like two steps forward and one step back, with rent control measures always being weaker than they want. Initially, they were offered rent control as something that local authorities could opt into for specified 'rent pressure zones'. None did. Then they won more comprehensive rent controls but only as a temporary measure, with permitted rent rises still too high. The fact that any rent controls at all are passed by the Scottish National Party, a party largely neoliberal in outlook, is a testament to the work of Scottish housing campaigners. They keep up the pressure, but do not make the mistake of trusting the SNP.

There is another variation in political institutions between the UK and Spain that makes a big difference to organising. The UK is one of the most politically centralised countries in the Global North. Relatively little can be achieved at the local or municipal level because local authorities have very little power. They cannot pass laws, they cannot significantly raise taxes, and they do not currently have substantive power over much of the housing system, except as regulator of it, with the regulations determined largely by central government in Westminster. Even local authorities' positions as landlords no longer gives them the power it once did, since it is so difficult to build new housing. Where once they built vast amounts of housing, they are now constrained by lending rules that prevent them from making big investments in social housing, despite the financial return being certain. What powers Westminster does choose to devolve, such as allowing local authorities to tighten landlord licensing regimes, always turn out to be toothless, particularly when executed with the budget constraints imposed by over a decade of 'austerity'.

Municipal governments in Spain, on the other hand, have significantly more power, and are able to execute real changes in the housing system. This is not uncontested: Catalonia's rent control measures were struck down by the courts as being beyond the powers of the regional government. But at least in Spain, power can be genuinely generated at the local level, which means that when tenant unions make demands on municipal governments, they have some chance of being heard. When left-wing organiser Ada Colau was elected as mayor of Barcelona, one of her first priorities was restricting short-term rental licences so as to curtail the rent-increasing spread of Airbnb in the city.

To stray once again into wider housing campaigning, the DWE expropriation campaign in Berlin rested entirely on local powers, which were also later challenged. But what could be mobilised at the local level was impressive. Berliners have a right to demand a referendum at the local level – something also true of many US cities but more unusual in Europe – and so the campaign mobilised initially around getting that referendum to happen. The campaigners had to collect thousands of signatures from across the city to get it on the referendum. This humdrum work of collecting signatures was for a surprisingly radical end: a demand that the city expropriate hundreds of thousands of apartments that had been privatised after the fall of the Berlin Wall. Having won the right to a referendum, the campaigners next had to win the referendum itself. This required an even bigger mobilisation to persuade voters to vote for expropriation. This was a people-powered campaign, requiring thousands of labour hours, and all based on the notion that there was some real power to be grasped at the municipal level. As I write, DWE has launched a final campaign for a binding referendum, having found that the politicians were too weak to implement the results of their non-binding referendum. Time will tell whether the campaign was right to bypass the work of building a more permanent neighbourhood-based tenant organisation. If the expropriation campaign finally wins, it may look like the right decision, but even then people may wonder 'what next?' If it does not win, it is likely many will ask why no permanent movement structure remains in the wake of so much labour.

Similar local city-level campaigns can and do happen in the US, being much more common than tenant campaigns aimed at Washington and its neoliberal impasses. This has resulted in many local victories, including winning rent control in cities across the country. St Paul, Minnesota, is thought to have the strongest rent control measures in the US – a cap of 3 per cent annual rent rises with no inflation adjustment – after a tenant organising drive that created the chance for citizens to vote in a local ballot to support the 'Keep St Paul Home Campaign'.

However, it should not be assumed that only stronger local democratic structures allow tenants to make their mark at the municipal level. In Kansas City, tenants organising with KC Tenants were able to build an incredibly strong reaction to the pandemic evictions crisis. A local eviction moratorium was initially achieved but was weakly supported and allowed to lapse well before the worst stage of the pandemic was over. Rather than working through the institutional structures that were clearly not designed to address such immediate emergencies, KC Tenants launched a relentless campaign of direct action against the courts that were evicting people. The evictions continued even after a nationwide 'evictions moratorium' took place, exploiting loopholes in the law. In response, KC Tenants doubled down on their direct action campaign, preventing court hearings from taking place by physically blocking courts or entering the courts in person or online and shouting for justice for tenants, thereby preventing hundreds of court cases from proceeding and blocking over 900 evictions in total. Through direct action they managed to effectively immobilise the court system that carried out evictions.

Still, even direct action tactics require the right local political conditions. The UK has such harsh anti-protest laws that many of the tactics of KC Tenants, such as going to the homes of judges, would be illegal, falling under anti-harassment laws. Blocking courts would result not only in punishment – a protester recently faced the threat of prosecution for merely holding a placard outside a UK court on the grounds that it 'perverted the course of justice' – but lead to injunctions to prevent further protest, against both individuals and groups. In addition, UK police have substantial powers to direct protestors to move or end their protests, arresting and fining them if they fail to obey police orders. These laws have been passed in a political environment where it appeals to a lot of voters to crack down on protestors who are seen as disruptive and as 'others' – imagined as 'work-shy hippies' or 'spoiled students'.

Decades of anti-protest legislation means that while UK tenant unions can and do use direct action, they have to do so more carefully than in countries with more entrenched protections for protest. ACORN UK found itself hit with a large fine when one of its campaigns was judged to amount to 'harassment' of the landlord against whom they were taking action. As I write, the UK government is rolling out 'Serious Disruption Prevention Orders', a new way of criminalising individual political organisers and activists. The criteria for serving them includes a person having two previous protest-related convictions. It is a fact of life for UK tenant organisers that they must contend not only with weak local democratic institutions, but with weakened democratic norms around protest. There is still space here for international learning: Los Angeles Tenant Union hold protests in defiance of the notoriously over-resourced Los Angeles Police Department (LAPD) by ensuring there are always children and older people protesting, which seems to make even the LAPD's behaviour more moderate. To get around the fact that some of their members are undocumented they sometimes hold rapid protests lasting only 30 minutes. By the time the police arrive, LATU are already gone.

All these political conditions can influence in quite profound ways how tenant unions see what they do. They must constantly be thinking about who the 'we' doing the organising consists of, and who the opponent is and whether the targets they have identified are within their power to pressurise. As an example, because UK tenant unions struggle to get anything positive out of local authorities, they have a tendency to fall into seeing them as an opponent, along with other landlords. Meanwhile in the US, where local institutions can sometimes be forced into yielding bigger concessions to tenant unions, developers – often most opposed to rent controls and spending lots on lobbying – get cited as the enemy more than in the UK.[1] Vancouver offers a counter-example: after years spent attempting to get city laws changed, Vancouver Tenants Union was worn out. Upon regrouping they wrote an assessment of their current situation:

> We've learned in the last five years that municipal elections have tended to prevent us from attaining the goals that we have collectively determined as a Union, by draining capacity from members.[2]

They had found local politics, dominated by a powerful real estate sector, to be a labyrinth that used up all their energy while delivering almost nothing for tenants. As a result, they have reoriented to long-term base-building.

Social democracy and socialist movements have been more successful in the UK than the US, which means that UK tenant unions are more likely to talk directly about 'the working class' being screwed by the landlord–tenant relationship. While LRU set out imagining that a 'tenant identity' could be constructed that would mobilise people, this has had limited appeal, probably because it is an identity many people wish to escape. So as time goes on, LRU talks more openly about class, though more hesitantly among newer members who are unaccustomed to that language. The notion of class position and being a tenant are then woven together, if rather incompletely, since the full class position of tenant union members can be rather complex. Any project to elevate tenants as a political force requires such close attention to the local political/cultural landscape.

TO PAY STAFF OR NO?

The staffing strategy of tenant unions, meanwhile, tends to be influenced by whether or not key organisers believe paid staff are *necessary* for building large-scale membership organisations, which tends to be influenced in turn by their experiences in their organising contexts. London Renters Union has recruited as many staff organisers as it can afford, its founders having discovered through previous experience that organising in diverse and atomised London was exhausting work for people to do in their spare time. There was a commitment to making the union's organising not just 'inclusive' in the sense of being welcoming to diversity, but making it actively anti-racist, and with a base within the poorest in London. They felt that only paid organisers could dedicate enough time to building the union in a way that fulfilled these ideals.

This LRU staffing comes with a certain ethos: it is not staff who are meant to run the union. Rather, the staff are meant to be subordinate to the elected Coordinating Group that is made up of unpaid members. This was a safeguard put in place by founder members who felt that in many large trade unions paid staff had accumulated too much power, and that this salaried staff power was a moderating influence on the unions, leading them to pursue low-risk strategies when what was needed was higher-risk radical action. Certainly, the staff in LRU have shown their value, their working weeks enabling them to do countless one-to-one meetings with members and to follow up with members struggling to be involved. Maintaining the ideal that staff in the union shouldn't accumulate power among themselves does get more challenging as more staff are recruited. It is difficult for staff not to exert any informal power in everyday work. They are the ones spending the most time doing organising and they sit together in an office where they can develop united positions on what needs to happen in the union. But the culture of the organisation overall is that staff are encouraged to stay aware of the need to consciously give power back to people and not take up too much space.

In his discussion of staff in the Bronx tenant organisation CASA, Glyn Robbins points out that staff are also susceptible to burnout, and that it can't be assumed they will have better welfare than stretched activists. He describes staff in a housing organisation as a 'mixed blessing' at best.[3] They can need management and support when struggling with their jobs and this becomes another task for others in the organisation. This is not to suggest that the problems outweigh the benefits. It feels true to me, in the context of the tough London organising landscape, that LRU couldn't do the type of organising it does with unpaid members alone. Nor is it the only union with that model: KC Tenants have also made their impact in Kansas City with a highly staffed model, with their $450,000 a year turnover mostly going to staffing – organisers, running a tenant hotline and some campaigning capacity.

In contrast, Crown Heights Tenant Union, after an initial experiment with paid staff from another organisation, has avoided recruiting any staff. In fact, CHTU is not even incorporated as an organisation, making it almost impossible for it to raise significant funding. Like Los Angeles Tenant Union, they feel that employing staff will inevitably introduce more moderate politics and compromises that will undermine the solidarity of organising. Brooklyn is as diverse a place to be organising as London, so it could be argued that CHTU offers proof that organising in a diverse city without staff is possible. But as discussed above, LRU and CHTU organise in quite different environments. Building-based organising provides new members with immediate commonality with their neighbours – commonality of experience and a common target. The more disparate organising in London means that commonality often has to be explicitly emphasised through education, or learnt through experience in the union.

Ireland's union CATU has taken a pragmatic middle path on staffing, with only five staff across the whole island of Ireland in which they organise. Staff in these mid-staffed unions are bound to be jacks-of-all-trades, able to turn their hand to anything the union needs, from negotiating with landlords to doing admin. Even if organisers are meant to be focused on recruitment and relationship-building, they are likely to have to provide back-up when unpaid members run out of steam. It is easy for a dispute with a landlord that drags on for too long to produce exhaustion or even boredom in the members leading the dispute. If it is a key dispute for the union, staff will feel they have to pick it up and push at those moments when energy in the union is low.

To some extent, as one organiser pointed out to me, the debate between staffed and unstaffed unions mirrors the debates between large, mainstream workplace unions and more aggressive anarcho-syndicalist unions about the dangers of bureaucratisation. But just as some small radical workplace unions have ended up employing staff for pragmatic reasons of avoiding burnout among members, so many tenant unions have chosen staff not because they want staff in a dominant role but because staffing feels necessary when members are overworking themselves to keep the union running. A successful tenant union must, by its nature, constantly maintain an organising infrastructure in the areas it covers, in order that disputes and campaigns can leap into action as required.

The question of staffing also relates to how fast a tenant union *wants* to grow, though not necessarily in the obvious way. CATU allowed itself a rapid growth model in order to spread across Ireland. It made it easy to set up local groups, allowing just 15 people to set up a CATU group in a locality – though a full branch requires 80 members. When it opened up to any new group wanting to get started during the pandemic, it couldn't possibly have staffed the level of rapid growth that occurred. Conversely, LRU, having committed to building roots in communities, has made it relatively difficult to start a branch: local members are expected to gather a hundred members and start providing 'member solidarity' and campaigning functions before they are allowed to convert into a branch. Since running a branch of LRU is a significant endeavour, it makes sense for each branch to get staff support. It may seem paradoxical that higher staffing levels and slower growth belong together, but LRU sees itself as getting deeply embedded in communities and the staffing strategy is a key part of doing so.

FUNDING AND ITS RISKS

Inevitably, staffing is closely related to another issue on which tenant union organisers have varying views: external funding. It is a defining feature of tenant unions that they ask their members to pay dues in the same way as a workplace union, though it is also true that, for the sake of inclusion, many tenant unions have free membership strata for people on very low incomes. While every tenant union organiser I have spoken to would – in theory at least – like to be entirely self-funding from membership dues, sometimes this has not felt possible. That particularly becomes the case if the model of the union is to employ multiple staff organisers. LRU fundraises quite significantly from foundations in order to maintain its staff level, though it has the ambition to increase the percentage of its income from membership dues. In the US, it can be more controversial to take institutional funding of any sort because cities already have foundation-funded housing groups that are expected by their funders to take more moderate approaches to organising and often end up being pro-developer. The UK does not have the same North American history of a large foundation-funded organising sector and so UK unions are happier to take the risks of having institutional links.

In Spain too there is less concern about the impact of institutional funders, in part, because Spain has some more radical institutions. The Sindicat de Llogaters has the help of a couple of staff paid by the Observatori DESCA, a human and economic rights foundation. But this becomes less surprising when we learn that the same organisation provided support to the mortgage-arrears campaign group PAH as it developed its model and grew. There seems little to fear from co-optation by moderate values when financial support comes through an organisation that helped shake up left organising across Spain and inspired housing organisers across the world.

The fear of many tenant unions which have decided to be funded only by dues is that, if they take external funding, they will have to moderate their claims, or come under pressure to work with landlords and developers rather than against them. This is a valid concern, particularly in the US institutional landscape. Part of what the Autonomous Tenant Union Network means by being 'autonomous' is precisely that they stay independent of non-profit and foundation funding. But in other countries where the foundation-funded organising sector isn't as hegemonic, it can seem less of a threat. All the new tenant unions have a mixture of more radical demands and more institutional demands that ask for government action. Often it is easy enough for tenant unions to approach more institutional funders by talking up their more moderate demands. They can and do tell funders they are offering 'renters rights' workshops and other non-threatening services, while remaining within the bounds of truth. The fact that a tenant union may also be committed to the downfall of capitalism needn't be mentioned in funding applications. Or like KC Tenants, they may simply find funders who are willing to take risks and agree to their money being used to help run high-impact direct action campaigns.

The approach of playing up the moderate aspects of tenant unionism may, we might guess, store up problems for the future, particularly if the union makes a big splash in the news and comes under increased scrutiny. It wouldn't be surprising to see more moderate funders pulling out if they felt the union's strategy or attitude to be too 'extreme', with ACORN in the US providing a sobering example. After right-wing attacks in the national media, including from influential politicians, ACORN's key funders got cold feet and withdrew, leading to the disintegration of what had been a significant community organising network.

THE MANY GOALS OF TENANT UNIONS

A key part of a union's strategy will be manifested in its stated goals. It should not be assumed that all tenant unions have the same goals, and the goals of tenant organisers can and do differ even within tenant unions. Divergent views about what the union should be doing are as common as in any medium-to-large political organisation. As one organiser said to me wryly, 'We try to stay comradely in expressing our differences and we *mostly* manage it.'

Before discussing housing justice goals, it is worth emphasising that tenant unions do not *only* have housing goals. It can be a part of their strategy to make links with other movements in order to help achieve anti-racist or environmental or inequality reduction goals. As the climate crisis takes hold, linking environment and housing will become increasingly strategically important. Unions might also have very localised political goals, or conversely, an ambition to broaden left-wing movements more generally – this last one in particular can be a key motivation for many organisers. Tenant unions can also be committed to a future of greater mutual aid of the sort that developed during the COVID-19 pandemic, wanting the working class to develop their own infrastructures to survive the coming crises.

The housing goals that unions do have can be broken down into three main categories: technical changes to the housing system that can be implemented by any government; social democratic housing solutions such as building publicly owned homes; and re-making housing by challenging capitalism itself. These varying goals or sets of goals usually coexist within a union, but they can create tensions, since they don't always fit together as well as some organisers would like. The first two are often complementary to each other: social democratic solutions can be seen as a subtype of technical solutions, being the subset that requires the redirection of more capital to achieve them.

Anti-capitalist politics, on the other hand, has the potential to create some rifts within a union. First, this comes in the form of a difference between libertarian-leaning socialists and state-centric socialists. Their ultimate goals can be different, and sometimes their methods and attitudes. At the risk of stereotyping their positions, while the former will emphasise democracy as means and ends, the latter will emphasise effective victory through taking state power. While both groups might think that collective ownership of housing is the ultimate anti-capitalist housing form, they might differ on, for example, whether that should happen through the state, or through independent co-operatives or other collectives, or through state funds appropriated to community ends.

Second, and perhaps more importantly, any sufficiently successful tenant union begins to recruit members who are not (immediately at least, and sometimes ever) disposed to anti-capitalism. I recall a meeting at which one organiser in LRU spoke, albeit hypothetically, about a future without paying rent at all. One new member stood up rather indignantly and said she thought that people should have to pay rent, taking a moral stance about the current system where the organiser had been hinting at a systemic revolution. Any tenant union aiming at mass organising will recruit members who are not anti-capitalist, some of whom will not become anti-capitalist even with attempts to educate them into radicalism. In theory, all tenant union members are aligned by the common interest of wanting better housing. But arguably, the alignment splinters if some members feel that housing can be fixed under capitalism – even if a more social democratic version of it – while others feel that housing crisis will never end until capitalism ends.

The ability to say the latter explicitly, or some version of it, can also depend on context. The Sindicat de Llogaters in Barcelona talk about taking *all* housing out of the market, but they do so in a context where left-wing ideas are much more widespread than in most countries of the Global North. They also don't talk about this exclusively in their political discourse. 'In the last year,' one Sindicat organiser told me, 'We've been creating the figure of the rentier as one of our opponents – those who don't live from work, and the culture that enables them.' This has presumably been put forward as a construction that even some capitalists and many sympathetic to capitalism could agree with.

This relates to another difference between and within unions: how much organisers want to *talk* about anti-capitalist politics, or whether they think their politics can be read in their actions and therefore require little explanation. This can come down to differences between particular organisers in the same union: some will openly talk about housing crisis being a result of capitalism, others will prefer to let people draw their own conclusions. But some unions do have policies they expect organisers to abide by. A Living Rent organiser told me, 'Our antagonist is those who profit from others' need for housing – structurally it is housing financialisation. If we expand to other issues, it would be capitalism. But we don't talk about capitalism or anti-capitalism because we want to get all renters on board.' This approach mirrors that of their partner organisation ACORN, but the potential splintering of alignments when a radical union recruits members who aren't radical leftists surely does not go away simply because anti-capitalism is not openly discussed.

Organisers' political leanings can also influence their views on how tenant unions should interact with the state. Some tenant union organisers insist that a 'right to organise', similar to the right to organise at work, is a vital part of their strategy. The state would be guarantor of this right, and might play the role of mediator where the right is under threat. Others downplay the importance of a right to organise, or simply see it as irrelevant, because one is always organising to undo power imbalances. One can even argue that creating a more comfortable environment in which to organise will only blunt the radicalism of a union, and looking at the older, established tenant unions in Northern Europe, such as in Germany or Sweden, one can certainly see evidence of this likely trajectory. For this reason, when Crown Heights Tenant Union was offered the chance to unite with a powerful campaign network to ask for the right to collective bargaining with the city authorities, they turned it down. They felt it would only hold them back from the battles they truly needed to win. In contrast, Vancouver Tenants Union is a key member of the British Columbia 'Rent Strike Bargain' coalition, which aims to win collective bargaining rights for rents, which they see as a key tenant protection.

The question of how to negotiate radical positions versus mainstream politics is also about how unions want to appear to members of the public and about the 'common sense' of the day. In CATU, there has been some discussion about how much to target housing owned by the charity sector. Some of this is low-quality temporary accommodation that is failing to meet the basic housing needs of its tenants. In one way, charities are easy targets because they can be more easily morally shamed into doing the right thing than a corporation. But others in the union are concerned that targeting charities will make the union look too hardline to the public and politicians. In the end, the role of the charities as landlords was decisive in determining the union's actions. As one organiser told me, 'The union model is, whoever is causing the problem, we go directly to them. We don't treat them differently. They're the ones managing the property. If a charity manages it, instead of a management company, we still hit the charity. If it's failing, if we have demands and we represent tenants, we don't mediate between tenants and social charity organisations ... Our model is community organising with direct action.'

HOW RADICAL CAN WE GO?

The issue of how to present a union's politics is implicitly a debate about how radical a 'tenant consciousness' organisers believe can be created and how much work that takes. If a strong consciousness can be built, then mainstream 'common sense' about who should or shouldn't be targeted can be overcome. Some organisers believe that a tenant class consciousness lurks just below the surface and tenants simply need to take action together to awaken it. Others believe that to build that tenant consciousness it will be necessary to do much political educational work. I would venture to say that, in what is still early stage organising for most of the new tenant unions, it is still something of an open question to what degree a particular 'tenant consciousness' can be formed, and even who will be included within the 'we' of organising. Tenant organising is not yet advanced enough that we can be sure what self-conceptions will arise, or what new collectivities will demand as they rise to more significant levels of success. Will unhoused people become a key part of the movement in some places? Will tenants begin to organise more with poor homeowners? And by what processes will new political consciousness emerge? The differences in whether unions see the need to do 'political education' presents us with a potentially interesting 'natural experiment'. The coming years will show the difference in outcomes between unions such as Living Rent that don't emphasise political education, unions like LRU that are developing a pedagogy of housing analysis, or unions like LATU that take a more Freirean, popular education approach to learning.

Los Angeles Tenant Union is the tenant union most drawn to radical pedagogy, and this leads to some interesting elements of its strategy to build power. It engages only minimally with institutions because its aim is subtly different from that of other tenant unions. While it does want to see improved housing in the here and now, organisers say its long-term plan is to create communities of solidarity that can ride out the coming storms of climate chaos and economic decline that the trajectory of global politics seems to make the most likely version of the future. This means the life of the union is imagined as being more than just a standard political space, rather it is a social space and a family space. One organiser told me:

> We were talking earlier of our union's orientation, not being one of like, tenants' rights, but of building life together, you know, towards unquestionably political aims ... I know a lot of working-class women with three jobs who make an enormous amount of time for the union, because it's life giving and it's, you know, it's social. It's when you come around it's food, it's like dinner, it's childcare. This is like, what you do after work because you come together in this space that is political, and it's a decision-making space. But it's also a social space, where we're taking care of each other's children, and we're making food together. And

we're sharing our life together. You know, we're having our one-year-old's birthday party at the end of the meeting, like, people make that space, people make that time.

Another organiser agreed and said that the tenant association, as the building block of the union, was not simply a political organising body but a social world too. The point is not to prioritise one over the other:

> [T]he two are completely dependent upon each other. And that's the kind of consciousness that I think as a union … that's the pedagogical work of the union, is to raise the consciousness about that interdependence, that you need the political struggle to help defend (and to help survive) the social life of that building. And the social life is what gives force to the political struggle.

This strong focus on the autonomy of the community, and upon radical pedagogy around that, is derived in part from a view of the state as essentially useless to solving housing crises. In Europe, where the ghost of social democracy lives on and governments can still be pushed to take positive action for their citizens, this hunkering down within community would seem to many organisers to be an overly pessimistic approach. Yet there are arguably many countries in which pessimism about the ability to capture the state for social good could turn out to be a good long-term strategic stance.

While they stand out in the latest wave of tenant union struggle, LATU are certainly not the only housing movement organisation to focus strongly on building communities of solidarity through radical pedagogy. Radical local neighbourhood associations (Atelier Populaire d'Urbanisme) in Lille do a lot of tenant organising but rarely see it as worthwhile to campaign beyond putting out some basic demands at local elections. They have been organising together for decades and are clear that their goals are the long-term ones of popular education and building solidarity. Through communities of learning and solidarity they will survive and thrive, whatever the political environment created by the French state.

A final type of tenant union strategy I want to discuss is one that not everyone would agree on as being a strategy. Many tenant unions aim to do prefigurative world-building, in which they try to create within their own organisation the world they want to see. There is a weak version of this that simply aims to address gender and racial disparities within the organisation, recognising that wider society is inflected with many injustices and that these need to be counteracted in order to build solidarity. But there is a stronger version too, more influenced by a libertarian left tradition, of trying to create an internal culture that aims to feel like a new society within the old. Gender, sexuality, race will all be actively addressed in attempting to level power relations between members. Some unions will want to deliberately create space for care and nurture within the organisation, or for experimentation with identity, or radical democratic forms. The tenant union can be envisaged as an almost utopian community, pushing back against the oppressive forces of the capitalist world outside. At an ATUN conference one organiser said:

> I have been thinking a lot about how the work of the tenants union is not just to effect change just outside our formation, but also to build some community in its own right – that the tenants union is my home.

For this organiser, that meant confronting the injustices of the everyday within tenant union organising itself. For many members, if a union were to win better housing, but minority groups felt uncomfortable or disempowered in their spaces, that would be a failure. But is this strategy? In his book *Hegemony How-to: A Roadmap for Radicals*,[4] Jonathan Smucker warns against social movement organisations focusing too strongly on internal culture and identity formation. He contrasts this with 'strategy', which he sees as being the concrete steps needed to gain power. One of the dangers of focusing too much on solving the world's problems within our own organisations, he claims, is that the strong internal culture this creates can separate us from other people and make recruitment too difficult. People enter a space that is aiming for complete justice within its own internal workings and it feels alien

to them, because people are behaving differently, using different language, to that which they are used to. This is *unstrategic*,
he points out, because unintentionally it has limited the growth of
many movement organisations. The strategic question we can ask
of internal union culture is does it actually win us better housing?

There is clearly a balance to be struck here: one wouldn't want
to return to the old left where sexual harassment, colonial attitudes and even outright racism went unchallenged. It's anyway no
good recruiting people with a passion for justice if you are going
to subject them to injustice. They simply won't stick around in the
face of such hypocrisy. This is why, at a minimum, tenant unions
in diverse cities must explicitly set out to address racial injustice,
both within housing and within housing organising. Those who
care about ending oppression will always feel strongly that certain
cultural changes are vital, and this will always be a part of radical
tenant organising. At the same time, getting involved in social
justice organising for the first time should probably not be mas-
sively culturally jarring for new tenant union members. It is only
possible to take a person so far in the space of one meeting – and
that's all that a tenant union will get before most new members
make their decision about whether to return. What this doesn't
mean is that those new members can't still be moved to radical
action. The action can and does emerge from the inherent conflict
in the tenant-landlord relationship. It has little to do with whether
someone self-identifies as 'radical'.

I can also hear in my head the voices of my friends in LATU,
who are insistent that tenant union organising is about the long
haul, about the achievements over decades, not years. The debate
about how far to model a new society within tenant union organising takes on a new cast if we consider that cultural change over
the long term is a part of what it will take to defeat the capitalist
mindsets of commodification and exploitation that have allowed
landlordism to thrive. Tenant unions may conceive of themselves
as fighting for better housing now, but most of them want a sub-
stantially better world in the future too. Maybe there is a strong
relationship within prefigurative strategies between cultural
change and economic change. Considered over a sufficiently long
timescale, autonomous tenant union strategies might presumably

aim to convert tenant union community into economic prefiguration, and thence a new economic future.

There is medium-term cultural work that can be done by tenant unions too: tenant organisers in Britain and Ireland often talk about delegitimising landlordism as a life choice. London housing organiser Nick Bano's recent book, *Against Landlords: How to Solve the Housing Crisis*,[5] attempts to give some theoretical underpinning to a landlord delegitimisation campaign. With two million landlords in the UK, all of whom have friends and relatives, this cultural shift will not be quickly achieved, but unions can at least start the delegitimisation narratives within their own organisations. Some new members of LRU find the ire directed at landlords to be 'too personal', but at least they understand this cultural difference within the union to be directly about housing.

Anyone who has watched a usually 'non-political' working-class person enter an 'activist' space for the first time knows there is also merit to Smucker's arguments. Taking seriously the idea of strategy versus internal culture means that organisations need to carefully think about the experience of new members. In London organising, working-class recruits sometimes look visibly uncomfortable at being asked to give their pronouns when introducing themselves. They simply haven't encountered such a practice before. To me that means not that we shouldn't do it – our trans or gender-non-conforming comrades may find it too important for it to be optional – but it does mean that other parts of the experience of joining should be more familiar to people in order to make them feel at home. An experienced activist may find it natural and caring to have an introductory round where people talk about how they are feeling that week, but it's good to understand that such a simple ritual for an old movement hand may be quite intimidating to new members unaccustomed to talking that way with strangers. It presumably shouldn't feel to new working-class members that they have to entirely leave behind their own culture in order to fully join the culture of a tenant union. A tenant union's strategy may involve cultural change, but it must also aim for broad-based recruitment, and that means not demanding that new members change things about themselves immediately. Going further than that, those organising with a base having a culture different to their own might find they need to change their own culture, particularly the instinct of professional class organisers to build bureaucratic organisations that mirror their workplace-learnt ways of being.

RENT CONTROL AS STRATEGY

The degree to which organisations develop prefigurative politics is a perennial dividing line on the left. There is, however, one policy demand on which most tenant unions agree because of its strategic power. I want to talk about it under the heading of strategy because it is the killer *strategic demand* of tenant organising, the one that brings together multiple beliefs, ideals and goals: the demand for rent control. Most tenant organisers want to see rent control implemented or, if they already have rent control, tightened up. It is a policy that works for the moderates (relatively speaking) of the tenant union world. But it works too for most of the radical organisers, for they see rent controls as a step towards the decommodification of housing. Moderates and radicals, anarchists and statist leftists can all unite around this one strategic demand: the rent is too damn high! Make it lower!

Rent controls are the top tenant union demand for an important reason: they are highly effective as a measure to improve the lives of tenants in the here and now. I touched on the benefits of rent control in the first chapter, but it is worth delving further into why this one demand brings so many tenant organisers together who are otherwise scattered across the left political spectrum. Rent is a simple transfer of wealth from those who don't own to those who do own. It is both the result of inequality and a multiplier of inequality. It is the drain that keeps millions of people in poverty. It is exploitation in the most basic sense, like the appropriation of the true wage of the worker, as landlords hold hostage a necessity of life. In fact, a company making 10 per cent profit may well only be keeping, say, 20 per cent of what a worker makes for them, while a landlord is often taking 50 per cent plus of a tenant's wages. That means that a tenant works half their week, from lunchtime on Wednesday, simply to support their landlord's lifestyle. The injustice of this transfer of wealth from poor to rich is clear to all tenant organisers. What is also clear is that the lives of tenants would become better in multiple ways if they had to pay less in rent. They would have more income for food, heating and other necessities, and yes, for a few more luxuries too. They may well be able to work less, particularly precarious workers and those doing punishing shift work. They would have more time for political organising, including tenant organising, and would be more able to remain in their own communities.

Rent control opponents like to claim that rent controls hurt tenants the most – as though they themselves are the true benefactors of tenants. They talk of disrepair, as though millions of people aren't living with disrepair already. Their argument that rent controls constrain supply and lower housing quality is only true of the most unsubtle versions of rent control, such as the UK's setting of a 'standard rent' in the early twentieth century, unchangeable from the date of the implementation of rent control. In practice, most versions of rent control allow, for instance, for small rises in rent when the landlord makes clear improvements to the property, or inflationary rises. They often allow too for new properties to collect a slight premium in rent to encourage building. But rent control opponents will ignore the decades of evidence that well-designed rent controls do work, that they don't constrain supply, that they do make ordinary people better off. Almost as though these opponents of rent control are not, in fact, the champions of the tenants! What rent control opponents really hate about this market intervention is that rent controls are a partial act of de-enclosure, making public once again a matter that they insist – to their own benefit – be arranged purely between private individuals or entities.

In order to achieve effective rent controls, it is necessary to shift the balance of power between tenants and landlords. That is why all tenant organisers see the benefit of what, on the face of it, looks like purely a policy matter. Mass organising is always about building power. Ordinary people organise because they don't have enough power. They do it because they are aware that the people who do have power are screwing them over. To a limited extent, landlords are organised themselves, and they will often become more so and pool money in order to fight off, say, a rent control measure. But landlords often don't need to be *very* organised, because the upper levels of society are riddled with landlords. They all understand each other without even having to discuss the issues. Tenants, then, must organise to wrest power from this culture of landlordism, and rent controls are the field on which this can happen. The landscape of power is inevitably exposed by a rent control campaign. Tenant unions' opponents must come into the open. They must state their case, however nonsensical and insincere it may be. The field of battle becomes clear, and tenants must unite if they are to win.

The final test of all tenant union strategies is whether they can make life better for tenants. Successful rent control campaigns can make an immediate impact. That doesn't mean tenant unions can demobilise once rent control is achieved: we know that it takes further tenant organising to ensure laws are enforced and tenants can stay put in the face of landlord aggression. We know too that landlords and property developers will work night and day to overturn the rent controls that have been won. Rent controls, once achieved, become the basis for future organising, as they are in Los Angeles and New York. Campaigns to win rent controls, to enforce them and to keep them will play a key part in the task facing new tenant unions in the coming decade: to grow bigger, build power, become mainstreamed, known and feared by landlords, all the while holding on to radical methods and visions. In the final chapter, we will discuss how tenant unions can win, not merely in the sense of giving respite or minor protections to tenants, but in the sense of transforming the housing system.

6

Towards the Rent Strike?

In 2023, York South-Weston Tenant Union launched what has turned into the largest rent strike in Toronto's history. Hundreds of tenants have taken action against rent increases and disrepair across multiple buildings, facing down two sets of profiteering landlords. Such large rent strikes are unusual outside of pandemic times, but Toronto's housing crisis has reached tortuous levels for the tenants involved. Tenants are drawing a line in the sand and building power to stop landlords going further. Sharlene Henry, a co-chair of the union and rent striker herself, said:

> We've had enough. Far too many corporate landlords are getting away with ignoring rent control while forcing us to live in unbearable conditions we can't even afford. They're squeezing us out of our homes despite record profits, and [Ontario premiere] Doug Ford is making it easy for them, but we won't. This movement will continue to grow until we win.[1]

As I write this book, the rent strike is ongoing, a shining example of multi-building organising.

Such inspirational struggles always raise the question of whether tenant unions can go further. All radical tenant organising will at some point hit upon the dream idea: a general rent strike. Enough tenants will go on strike to cause financial distress to multiple landlords and genuinely shake the political establishment. How generalised the rent strike can become is an open question. Anyone organising even a section of one city, such as London's East End rent strikes in the twentieth century, would shake up the politicians. If we could organise all tenants in one city to go on strike, we would create an inspiring example of organising that would resound down through generations. But what if we could go further? Is a national rent strike possible? Is a multi-landlord international rent strike possible? These are genuine open questions until they are tried, but every tenant organiser has wondered whether the opportunity and means might present themselves for taking the strike beyond a few individual blocks. The COVID-19 pandemic momentarily raised hopes that enough people might be angry enough with their landlord's continued demands for rent while they were unable to work that a truly huge, coordinated rent strike might break out. In the end, most governments of the Global North cannily put in place just enough pressure valves – increased welfare payments, eviction moratoriums – to head off such an eventuality. To look at what a (at least partly) generalised rent strike might look like, we must look to those who have organised before us.

At the outbreak of the First World War, there was a sudden and unprecedented demand for new ships for Britain's navy and merchant navy, and for munitions. The factories and Clyde shipyards of Glasgow pulled in thousands of new workers to provision the war. Local landlords decided to capitalise on this war effort by putting up their rents – not exactly 'in response to market pressures', though they might have claimed that. In those days, the big landlords of Glasgow could all sit in a room together, and they often did, forming a monopoly from the point of view of poor workers. So the landlords sat in a meeting and decided that the war and the efforts of those fighting the war was a good opportunity to hike their rents.

But the people of Glasgow were in no mood for this war profiteering at their expense. In particular, the women of Glasgow decided they would not accept it. A rent strike was called. As one striker, Helen Crawfurd, later explained:

> The Glasgow Women's Housing Association took up this issue, and in the working class districts, committees were formed, to resist these increases in rents. Cards, oblong in shape, were printed with the words 'RENT STRIKE. WE ARE NOT REMOVING.' and placed in the windows of the houses where rent increases were demanded.

This quote was found in archives by historian Catriona Burness, and what I love about it is the casualness of the phrase 'committees were formed'. These working-class women already knew how to organise, perhaps having learnt from the partners in trade unions, or perhaps having been involved in unions themselves, or other forms of association. This is a strike that came out of a period of working-class struggle that was to some extent suppressed by the outbreak of war, but here arose again, quickly and efficiently adopting organisational forms that had already seen some success. The presence of the Independent Labour Party and its organising networks may have played some part, but the women acted of their own accord out of their own organisational capacities.

The strikers set up a bailiff resistance network across multiple tenement blocks, ringing bells to warn if any bailiff approached, then gathering to physically prevent evictions happening. This sometimes involved pelting them with flour bombs and other food-stuff, a level of aggression which puts the passive resistance of most eviction resisters these days in the shade. There was also significant interaction between the housing organising and trade unionists, with the men coming out to support the strikers when called. But fundamentally, the women were in charge of this campaign, and considered their actions legitimate on the grounds that it was their role to defend their households.[2] This was a struggle for a decent standard of living, for their children to be able to eat; it was a struggle of necessity, and their commitment to it was accordingly unwavering. The strikers refused rent rises for months, and they kept the bailiffs at bay, with 20,000 tenants on strike at the peak. Strike activity began to spread across the country again, reignited by the fiery example of the women of Glasgow. The tenants were not only winning their own battles but were proving the strength of collective action, and that scared the government. Within a few months, the government had passed the UK's first rent control Act.

An important postscript to this story is that it wasn't only the Glasgow rent strikes that won the UK's first rent control. David Englander, historian of Britain's tenant struggles, is always at pains to point out that there had been a huge wave of rent strikes across much of the UK, of which Glasgow was only the culmination. What looked like a victory for Glasgow's strikers was in fact a victory for a whole movement of tenants. In the years that followed, rent control was kept in place by further agitation among tenants, who kept alive the spectre of 'unrest' that haunted a government that kept a keen eye on revolutions and uprisings on the continent. This constantly reinvigorated housing struggle ultimately led to several waves of public housing construction. If anything, it was public housing as much as rent control that became the great legacy of the rent strikes. Across the UK, vast areas of privately owned land were compulsorily purchased for the construction of millions of municipally owned homes. This legacy has been undermined by years of neoliberalism but by no means has it been entirely lost. To many visitors to London, it is astonishing to discover that there is significant public housing even in wealthy areas of central London. One only needs to take a step outside of central London to Southwark to discover the highest percentage of social housing in England and one of the largest areas of public housing in Western Europe. This is where rent strikes can take a country: millions of people living in better conditions than their parents could have imagined.

This history of housing victories is a key inspiration to tenant organisers in the UK, though clearly the victories of the past cannot be simply repeated. We live under new conditions, so something new will have to happen to really shake up housing in countries of the Global North. But it is worth asking what can be learnt from this previous wave of tenant struggle. First, it is clear that it did not emerge from nowhere but rather from decades of working-class organising. Second and relatedly, organising institutions such as trade unions had taught thousands of people organising methods. Third, it did require a prong of the movement to be thrust upwards into political institutions, if with the compromise of foregoing the possibility of more revolutionary changes. Fourth, it required communities of solidarity to be constructed on a scale we rarely see in the Global North these days – though the movements of, say, India or Brazil are larger again than anything ever seen in the UK. And fifth, it required the ruling class to be genuinely fearful of what 'the masses' might do to them.

I will discuss in turn how each of these might be translated into the present day, but first I want to reiterate both what is at stake and the challenge that tenant unions are facing. Our ability to confront housing crisis will determine not only our own quality of life but the quality of life of our children. Housing decisions made now will echo down through generations, making lives better or worse, depending on our decisions. In the UK, 'build-to-rent' properties that the developers never plan to sell, only let out at high market rents, are set to hit a million units by the end of the decade. A lack of public housing takes many years to rectify. In 2024, the National Child Mortality Database in the UK estimated that in the previous five years, homelessness and temporary accommodation had killed 55 children, the majority under the age of one. It would be naive to imagine this can't get worse. It almost certainly will get worse before it gets better, and it will not get better unless mass movements force the hands of those in power.

Also at stake is the ability of differing sections of society to democratically engage with each other. The degradation of large parts of the population by rentierism in order to swell the coffers of a smaller number is not just about financial inequality. It is about a society in which those at the top are not able to see those below them as fully human and deserving of rights. If this sounds hyperbolic, consider that throughout this book I have presented examples of the contempt for tenants that abounds among landlords and their agents. Consider the hatred and legal aggression frequently directed at the unhoused in the US, a country that prefers imprisoning its poor to housing them. If these divisions become embedded further, the economic gulfs will inevitably become wider political gulfs. The new enclosures will continue unabated, driving a large part of society into pauperism while a few live in comfort.

Nor do I want to romanticise the oppressed tenant by saying that they will only ever demand a more egalitarian society. Elements of the ruling class will almost certainly have success in turning one set of tenants against another, opening the way for far-right governments. It is likely that housing crisis has already been a strong factor in the swing to the far right in many countries. The UK's recent far-right anti-refugee riots saw the deployment of the familiar trope that refugees and other migrants were 'taking council houses that should go to "real" English people', and anger at the hotel accommodation of refugees paid for by the government that is failing to house citizens. It is a certainty that opportunistic politicians will continue to blame migrants or some other oppressed group for people's poor housing conditions. We live in a time where the vast inequalities caused by Silicon Valley have produced the insult of 'NPC', or non-player character, thrown around at opponents on social media. People are accusing each other of being barely human unthinking sheep, or like a video game character, often in the same breath praising Silicon Valley billionaires who they believe to be the 'real' characters with drive and entrepreneurialism to usher in a new world. This is about the contempt that billionaires have for ordinary people infecting many of those ordinary people who have a desire to see themselves as superior. There is a dark future without tenant organising where tenants become more widely understood as 'NPCs' or 'marks', and even tenants who believe they will one day escape renting into ownership will sneer at those they believe will never escape.

A future without tenant movements holds some certainties and many hazards. The certainties are poverty, sickness, mental ill-health, malnutrition, abuse and despair – a worsening of the current state of housing crisis. The hazards are a public sphere dominated by the powerful – by landlords and their allies and their lackeys – and a politics that offers only division and violence. This is the likely end point of accumulation by dispossession, endless competition in which the many losers are held in contempt, and the failure of already-waning democratic institutions.

Thankfully, a movement of tenant unions is rising. It is growing year by year, and shows no signs of tiring. It resists these tendencies, creating unity, solidarity, self-respect and a more democratic society in the struggle for better housing. But before we think about what victory for tenant unions will look like, we need to delve a little deeper into the economic and political conjuncture. We need to understand the full extent of the challenge. We must take a tour through the opposition, and in doing so spend some time talking about homeowners, who are not exactly the opposition, but due to their position have the capacity to act as a major bar to change.

THE RENTIER'S WORLD

There are two major blocs who benefit from the current state of the housing market. They are wildly different groups of people, yet only one of them will be talked about by politicians because only one of them is likely to elicit public sympathy. 'Ordinary home-owners', as a politician might refer to them, form the largest bloc of voters in many countries across the Global North. Neoliberal trade regimes have brought flatlining wages, underemployment and savage de-skilling to much of the economy, but those who owned homes could hold their breath and survive, for the value of their property was going up. This not only gave them a valuable asset to leave their children but enabled them to release cash to fund their lifestyles through various means: downsizing, remort-gaging or moving to a cheaper area. It is an oft-forgotten part of the gentrification story that plenty of ordinary homeowners have benefited from it. Far from feeling 'driven out' of an area, many willingly sold a $500,000 house they bought for $100,000 so they could move to an area where $250,000 could buy an equally good house, elevating their lifestyles by going mortgage-less or taking a pile of spare cash in the process. This is not in any sense a defence of gentrification, but we would do well to remember that gentri-fication processes might struggle to get the political support they do if they were entirely negative for ordinary people. Whether or not one feels 'driven out' of an area by rising house prices depends in part on whether one minds moving. Sometimes people will-ingly move from city to suburb or suburb to small town, even as others feel forced out and traumatised by the destruction of their communities.

So intense have been the capital gains of homeowners in many countries that economists have begun to talk of 'asset-based welfare' regimes. That is to say, houses have become the main defence for individuals against the vagaries of the economy, the erosion of the welfare state and the weakness of pensions. Gov-ernments then seek to support house prices either directly, or indirectly through allowing mortgage innovation, well knowing that the more money can be borrowed against housing, the higher the prices go. Welfare continues to be slashed, to little comment or applause from the mainstream media. This works okay for those who own a house, and leaves nothing for those who don't. It also means that if house prices don't go up, homeowners suddenly feel their vulnerability in economies hollowed out by years of de-industrialisation, de-skilling, precarity and low wages. And so it becomes a political imperative to keep house prices high. This is what an entire generation of young people faces: a political system working deliberately against them, while their elders upbraid them in mainstream media for perceived 'luxury' expenditure. Bad-faith claims that young people are unable to buy houses because they buy avocado toast or have too many streaming subscriptions have become a joke among younger generations. But as tenants' voices are silenced and the absurd game of blaming the victim continues, the joke has turned rather bitter.

Which brings us to the second group who have benefited from ever-rising house prices: the class of people who own assets over and above their own house, of which landlords form the section that invests in housing. This is the group of people the politicians don't talk about so much, because they form the upper section of society and those who defend them find it harder to cast themselves as 'of the people'. They include corporate landlords, large-scale investors in stock markets, fund managers, large commercial landlords, developers and even wealthy professionals who siphon off sections of their high income into assets. An economy that keeps asset prices high often keeps house prices high too. Entire sections of the financial sector are dedicated to servicing these asset owners.

Plenty of people are making money directly from rent or indirectly from the rentiers. Their voice is very much heard in the upper halls of power, even if the politicians don't wish to talk about them. In fact, they often sit in the upper halls of power. But what is also true is that, compared to previous gilded ages, asset ownership has been significantly democratised. This bloc is not even close to being as large as the homeowner bloc, but neither are we talking simply about the 1 per cent. We live in an age where everyone who has the cash or credit available has been encouraged to become an asset owner[3] and buy themselves some shares on the stock market. In some countries, the UK in particular, even landlordship has become widespread, with around two million landlords in a country of 60 million people. The one set of landlords that politicians will openly defend is the very real figure of the grandmother who owns two homes in order to supplement her meagre pension, or the 'mom-and-pop landlord' as they are described in North America. Despite this, the asset-owning bloc is still small enough, and unlovable enough, that few politicians are willing to appeal to it directly or very often. If we separate voters into a homeowner bloc, a landlord bloc and a tenant bloc, the landlords form by far the smallest bloc even in the UK, and in many countries landlords are almost insignificant as a voter bloc.

I have depicted landlords as only part of a larger asset-owning class because the fate of all asset owners is intertwined. This does not mean that house prices and stock market prices always rise together (historically they don't), but there are certain interventions that government can make, such as the quantitative easing that happened in response to the 2008 financial crisis, which benefited all asset owners, regardless of asset type. Both house prices in the landlord investor market and stock market prices strongly benefit from the investor confidence that comes from governments who treat private property as inviolable. We take it as read these days that all rich-country governments elevate private property protection as their *raison d'être*, but we only have to go back to the 1960s to see a highly capitalist country like the UK seizing vast sections of its cities and countryside from private owners in order to put an end to slums and build public housing. The avoidance of such governments in the future is a key political goal of all types of asset owners. This is one reason that hating on landlords will never be enough for tenant unions to win systemic change. It is not the landlords who are the true guarantors and defenders of the current regime, it is a wider asset-owning class whose centre is the financial services bloc.

These are the power blocs, then, that tenant unions today must confront. I have described what Antonio Gramsci would call 'the relation of forces' of the housing system here because they are the key to understanding the different choices faced by both tenants and governments. Governments tend to lean against the rights of tenants for two important reasons: that the homeowner voting bloc must be kept happy, and that the rights of asset owners must be held inviolable if they are to keep on board a broad array of powerful interests which may well fund them, and with whom they are more likely to identify than with tenants. That is to say, governments have one big, sort-of-democratic, reason to ignore tenants, plus one big, very undemocratic, reason to ignore tenants. If asked why they are ignoring tenants' needs, they are likely to refer to the homeowner bloc, and the importance of growing it, as the main reason, knowing that this has a more democratic tint to it. Arguably, the real reason is that they lean towards protecting asset owners at all costs, even to the detriment of the majority.

Moments do arise when particular governments – even rightwing ones – feel the need to woo the tenant voter bloc, but this must always be done, governments believe, without upsetting asset owners. Over all of these fissures hovers a deeply embedded market ideology that allegedly wishes to minimise government interference in the economy, though, as the 2008 financial crisis showed, this belief turns out to be extremely flexible when the interests of the wealthy are threatened. The 'common sense' among most major political parties in the Global North is that housing should primarily be provided through the market, with as little intervention from government as possible. The fact that these beliefs don't shift in the face of the transparent failure of this approach is testament to the powerful blocs that stand to benefit from the continuation of the status quo. These alignments naturally extend into the media class, as illustrated by the tale above of LRU member Kirsty having to face down a news presenter landlord talking nonsense about 'unqualified' tenants.

This set of political forces around 'housing crisis', then, is something of a Gordian knot for tenant unions to face. The approach that appears the easier one is to slice off the landlord bloc from both homeowners and the wider asset-owning class and target them with measures such as rent controls or property taxes. It can certainly lead to some quicker wins to do this than to take the difficult path: to face down the entire asset-oriented economy and the flows of capital that dominate real estate. Yet countries such as France and Germany stand as a warning against the easier solution: they have rent controls, they have secure tenancies, they have established tenant representative organisations that act aggressively against bad landlords, yet the price of housing keeps inflating and precarity of housing continues. In Berlin, once a global centre of squatting and anti-capitalist DIY culture, activists admitted to me that they were losing the battle against gentrification. The money keeps pouring in, prices keep going up and rent control is a finger in a dyke that keeps bursting in different places. The wider asset-owning class has not been challenged, capital has not been redirected from the private sector into the public sector or community ownership at scale. Tenants struggle to keep their heads above the water and their quality of life, or dream of a better quality of life, slips away.

AGAINST THE POWER OF CAPITAL

In the Greek legend, the Gordian knot is not quite irresolvable. It is undone by Alexander the Great shearing straight through the knot with a sword. Tenant unions are the sword that cuts the knot of housing crisis, not with violence, but through constructing tenants as fighting collectives that can slice through existing power blocs and electoral games. But to think about tenant problems as housing problems gives only a part of the picture, for in order to cut the knot, an entire way of doing politics must be challenged. For governments to accept that markets are failing to provide housing, they must accept that markets are failing in many ways. The resolution to never-ending housing crisis requires the mobilisation of vast resources in the interests of ordinary people, and thus can only come about through the end of the globalised neoliberal regime and the rentier economy it has created.

This clarifies for tenant unions some strategies that cannot bring about systemic change. Localised anti-gentrification protests, history shows, rarely achieve more than the saving of a particular building or community asset. Small islands are saved among seas of capital, and that capital is still directed by a particular stratum of people in their own interests. The point of saying this is not to be discouraging, it is to make clear the struggle that lies before tenant unions. They can only win through understanding the terrain upon which they are fighting. This includes a clear-eyed view even of the examples of organising that we love, such as local anti-gentrification organising. Gentrification that causes dispossession can rarely be beaten at the local level, though local fights can certainly be learning spaces for activists. That is the lesson of Berlin, which has had the strongest anti-gentrification organising in Europe, but has nonetheless gone from cheapest capital for housing in Western Europe to overheated property market in the space of a couple of decades. Targeting authorities that don't have significant taxation or legislative powers is another tactic with limited power. The demonisation of local authorities for being complicit in gentrification in the UK has not led to one with less gentrification. Those authorities don't have the power to redirect capital, and as bad as their decisions might sometimes be it is important to be clear about their limits so that energies can be directed towards the centres of power that can redirect capital.

To understand what victory looks like, tenant unions, whatever their varied strategies, are developing a sophisticated analysis of the fundamental problem. It is not corrupt local government or young professionals moving into new areas, or new coffee shops pushing out older businesses. Even the corruption appears more like a symptom of a system twisted by rentierism. On the systemic level, the problem is the vast streams of capital flowing into property that have taken it out of our hands. To create real change, those streams have to be either stopped or redirected and rentierism directly challenged. The capital flowing from liberalised banking regimes and easy credit needs to be either stopped by legislation or scared out of the sector. The property investments from rich people need to be stopped either by taxation or by legislation to discourage ownership except when occupying. The investments going into developments need to be redirected, through taxation or other means, towards new public housing controlled by those who live in it. Capital, for as long as we have a system where it dominates, needs to be redirected away from assets towards productive, sustainable industry. This end to rentierism looks, at the very least, like strong social democracy at central government level, and it may need to move beyond that. It means the end of the neoliberal era, and the defeat of the rich who have successfully argued for decades that their investments are more important than our homes. It would clearly require radical realignments of the political landscape on more than just housing issues.

Those most likely to talk about a 'housing movement' are usually left-wing activists who are invested in a broader anti-capitalist or socialist identity. Many of them, when I have asked, admit that they fell into housing campaigning by accident or through pragmatism, and that what they really want to see is an entirely new economic system. In as far as there is a housing movement, then, it often appears to be a sub-movement within a broader movement of people wanting to end capitalist social relations. But these committed organisers aim to recruit to their movements those who are not anti-capitalist, who simply want better housing. Perhaps it makes sense to call this hybrid group of committed anti-capitalists plus housing organisers with more moderate politics a movement in itself. Yet, arguably, the housing movement only attains coherent politics when hitched to a broader vision of how economic relations should work.

The systemic nature of the problems, alongside high home ownership in some places, means that tenant unions know they have to work with others to build the power they need. As they grow and develop into networked actors within broader movements, tenant unions will be uniquely positioned to spearhead the fight against the rentier economy. In addressing housing crisis, a thousand other problems of our societies will be addressed too. An organiser with Barcelona's Sindicat told me, 'We've been talking more and more with labour unions and other kinds of organisations because we know that this [the loss of spending power to rent] is something that is going to explode sooner rather than later in Spain and, you know, Europe.'

MOVEMENTS THAT WIN

To imagine tenant union victory, let's return to the factors of success of the rent strikes in Glasgow and the rest of the UK in the early twentieth century. The first we mentioned was that the rent strikes emerged from decades of working-class organising. A culture of organising already existed in Glasgow at the time the war struck and intensified housing crisis. Those women who sprang into action had all encountered organising before, either directly or through their menfolk. At present, most countries of the Global North are far from having a culture of organising. As a culture we are still reeling from the success of hyper-individualism and the culture of winners and losers. In order to embed real cultural change, it is vital that it is not only tenants who are organising. Community organising and workplace organising need to be happening at scale across society. People need to be moving seamlessly between workplace organising, community organising and tenant organising, so that the skills needed in any given housing confrontation are there without the need to start from scratch. Tenant unions will play a key part in building this culture of organising, though they all understand that they can't do so alone.

What tenant unions can also do is contribute significantly towards the second factor behind the success of those Glasgow rent strikes: build organising institutions that teach organising methods to many thousands of people. London Renters Union, like other tenant unions, has a conscious aim to train as many members as possible in organising methods. It would be very useful to tenant unions if trade unions were also taking the same approach. For some years I have been a member of one of the UK's large conglomerate unions, one of two that have the majority of union members in the country. In my experience, they do not offer any organising training to rank and file members, nor have I witnessed any organising by them in workplaces. Some would say that it is unlikely they will ever again train large numbers of members in organising, since there is nothing more troublesome to the leaders of the big unions than an active rank and file. Smaller, more radical challenger unions attempt to step in where these large unions have failed, but it will be a long time before they have the membership of the large unions. I would like to be less pessimistic than those who say the big unions will never offer significant organising training again. At some point, their dwindling membership may drive them to take drastic action out of a desire for self-preservation. In the meantime, new institutions of organising must be set up wherever possible.

The third factor in the success of the Glasgow rent strikes seems to many people to be a mixed blessing: that the labour movement, of which the rent strikes were a kind of spin-off, sent their representatives to Parliament, first. through disparate party organisations, then through the Labour Party. At the time it seemed important to the movement to have their people inside the political institutions arguing for them, and it is difficult to imagine that the incredible waves of public housing construction that gripped the UK mid-century would have been possible without that political intervention.

It can be argued that the British social democratic compact that was reached, not just in housing but in healthcare, wages and wider social welfare, also headed off the possibility of more radical change. Some people argue that this was precisely its purpose. And yet it is not clear that, absent the social democratic settlement, a revolution would have gripped the UK. The General Strike of 1926 laid bare the dividing lines between those who did and didn't want to wield strikes as a weapon to challenge the government, and it turned out that those who did were a minority. Even much of the labour movement shrank away from truly trying to challenge establishment rule, and many trade union leaders spent their time trying to contain the 'radicals' in their unions. In the wake of the strike, the government saw an opening for anti-union legislation and took it. But they also built housing.

One only needs to look at the US to see that there was an even worse way for governments to deal with a powerful labour movement: kill and imprison thousands of union organisers and members, murdering them either directly with state agents or indirectly through outsourcing the work to unaccountable militias like the Pinkertons. In the UK, the Churchills of the upper classes would have loved to have taken this route, and from time to time they were let off the leash, as in South Wales in 1910–11. The fact that there were other elected politicians in positions of power who were not inclined towards violence against the poor seems important. A narrative of radicalism betrayed is attractive, but it seems likely that the social democratic settlement that was achieved was the limit of what was possible for UK movements at the time, and that having movement actors within Parliament was key to the victory.

We can look to a later era too for an example of successful reworking of political institutions: the Greater London Council

(GLC) in the 1980s became a hotbed of radical municipalism, led by Ken Livingston, John McDonnell and others. This government for London attempted to conceive of itself as a convergence point for social movements. Radical banners often hung around the GLC building, and social movement organisers were invited inside to help devise policy. Among its achievements is the creation, in response to community campaigning, of Coin Street Community Builders, a predecessor to Community Land Trusts that still controls a significant block of land on the South Bank, right in the heart of London. This prime real estate is home to hundreds of low- to middle-income tenants who are able to live here in housing co-operatives because the land was decommodified. It took a mixture of movements and formal political institutions to make it happen.

It is also true that the GLC offers a harsh lesson: that sometimes winning paints a target on your back. Thatcher hated the social movement municipalism being projected from County Hall, just over the river from Westminster, and at the peak of her power she simply abolished the GLC. The movements that fed into it were not strong enough to defend it. We can now understand why UK local authorities are as disempowered as they are: they have so little power to address housing crisis precisely because that was what central government intended. They were decimated in order to fend off the 'threat' of left-wing municipalism, not only in London but in Liverpool, Manchester and other cities. Yet for all that it was finally defeated, the GLC still shines as a beacon of what can be achieved when movements surge up into institutional spaces.

This line of reasoning comes with a warning for those who would throw themselves directly into party organising, and no doubt this would be foregrounded by tenant unions like LATU and some in CHTU who doubt the logic of engaging with formal political institutions. From Greece to Germany to Spain, left-wing parties in recent years have found themselves ostensibly in power, only to discover that capital still rules the world. The bright stars of the Corbyn and Sanders moments in the UK and US, respectively, show us the problems of tying political projects to particular left-wing politicians. The risks and limits of the strategy were deftly described by Sai Englert in an article for grassroots organising strategy website *Notes From Below* that attempted to assess the political moment as those stars were dying:

> The current renewal of a basic set of social democratic demands for reform – as captured in the Corbyn project or the movement surrounding Bernie Sanders in the US – represents therefore all the excitement and the limitations of the current moment. On the one hand, the return of struggle – however limited – and the temporary revolts against the status quo point to growing discontent with the state, the ruling class, and their dominant ideological approaches for the last four decades. At the same time, however, there has not been a rebuilding of working class power from below. Unions remain weak, their rank and file broadly unconfident and disorganised, while huge swathes of the labour movement – particularly amongst young workers and across the private sector – are not unionised at all. Community self-organisation is largely non-existent, as are the collective forms of solidarity that emerge from it.[4]

The lesson of the failed European left-wing parties is that left-wing politicians in power are often useless without a big, mobilised base encompassing a significant proportion of society. This positions tenant unions as part of the solution to the left's depressing inability to cut through neoliberal alliances. The above was written in 2020 and I hope that, as I write this in 2024, the writer is feeling more optimistic. Tenant unions have been on the rise over those years, and it is no longer possible to say that community self-organisation is 'largely non-existent' in the UK and the US. Everywhere that a tenant union springs up, so does the collective solidarity that is key to large movement-building, and to building coalitions that can exert real power over capital.

This brings us to the fourth factor in the success of the Glasgow rent strikes: large-scale communities and networks of solidarity, covering large geographic areas. There is no shortcut to building these when society is so atomised, in many ways seeming to be only now hitting Peak Individualism. Most people in countries of the Global North have – with some exceptions among migrant groups – zero experience of collective organising against power, and that cannot be fixed in a hurry. A few islands of intense organising in a handful of big cities is unlikely to cut it. If that sounds depressing it is not meant to be, and LATU certainly don't see it that way. An organiser with LATU explained to me their conception of time and movement-building:

> But I think this is like, a slow ... we're only seven years old, Jacob, I think about the MST, they've been at it, what for 45 years? So, you know, we're kind of just at the beginning – baby steps.

MST is Brazil's Landless Workers Movement, whose tactic is land occupations that improve the lives of its members, and whose strategy is organising for as long as it takes to build power. It is an organisation with decades of experience in developing both material resources for members and political strategies. Its support to political parties, including the leftist Workers Party, is conditional and always about pushing the parties to the left. The MST, at 1,500,000 members, is only one of various large-scale organising vehicles in Brazil. It participates in and helps create a social movement base in Brazil that is too powerful to be entirely ignored, even by ruling-class parties. That LATU organisers chose to refer to MST reflects not only their sense of time but their ambition in movement-building.

One organiser in CHTU, on the other hand, told me they took inspiration from the labour movement. This is a more common movement for tenant union organisers to cite, being the large-scale movement that most people in the Global North are most familiar with. An LRU founder told me:

> [The LRU project being] about building power – it resonated with me because it wasn't present in other activism. And I had been involved in ... having lost several battles. We got that idea of power building from very long term history – the history of the labour movement and community organising.

Both examples give us a glimpse of the scale that many tenant union organisers are thinking about when they organise. Whether or not they have studied the Glasgow rent strikes, they will be aware that it can't only have been Glaswegians who won such a victory. They understand that organising in a single district or city will help individuals, but that to aim for systemic change requires a truly grand vision. Large percentages of society are going to have to become organised to shift the embedded neoliberal consensus. One could almost think in terms of a culture shift, a normalisation of organising rather than it being a niche activity. Endeavours such as the Autonomous Tenant Union Network (ATUN), and the more recent US-based Tenant Union Federation, aim to be not just ways of linking up lonely islands of tenant union activity, but a way of spreading tenant unions across all of North America. In 2024, anti-capitalist tenant unions from around the Global North met in Barcelona for the first time in an international tenant union convergence. They produced a declaration which included the aim of establishing 'a permanent space of cooperation and communication between tenant unions from different countries', including working towards inclusion of organisers from the Global South in order to achieve solidarity of truly global reach.

As part of extending their societal and geographic reach, most tenant unions are also interested in alliances with other organisers: trade unions as already mentioned, but beyond that anti-gentrification organising, climate organising and organising for justice for oppressed groups. It's easy to see that as extreme weather continues to hit us due to climate change, the synergy between climate organising and housing organising will only increase. Already in the UK, spin-offs from Extinction Rebellion, Insulate Britain and Housing Rebellion have sought to highlight the link between climate justice and our living conditions. These links between movements often already exist in the Global South and it is likely that such interaction will emerge on an increasingly international level.

The fifth factor in the victory of the Glasgow rent strikes was that the governments of the day genuinely feared the grassroots activity of the masses. As revolutionary turmoil broke out across Europe, peaking with the October Revolution, governments became frightened that their people too would turn against them. They were genuinely scared of the civil unrest that broke out on the streets of Glasgow as tenants fought bailiffs and protesters fought police, particularly when it spread to other cities. Initially, the government just didn't want anything to undermine its stupid and catastrophic war efforts. It did what it had to do to calm down the civil unrest. But interventions in housing continued through the following decades as governments understood that the masses they feared would be stirred up for as long as housing remained expensive, insecure and inadequate.

The UK was not the only country where tenant activity was scaring governments. The Swedish tenant movement was engaging in highly disruptive 'blockades' of properties where the landlord had put up rents too much, and called upon trade unions – with some success – to stand in solidarity with them to blockade businesses too. On the back of such activity the Swedish tenant movement became the most powerful in Europe, with tenant unions having the ear of governments for decades to come.

Piven and Cloward, in their classic book *Poor People's Movements: Why They Succeed, How They Fail,*[5] claimed that efforts by the poor to organise up to state level are inevitably co-opted. Sufficient control can never be exerted from the base to really control politicians who are supposedly 'of the people'. They concluded that the best method for movements of the poor to get what they need in a 'democratic' country like the US is to split moderate voters by becoming ungovernable, to disrupt everyday life until one party concedes – or cracks under the strain, forcing their opposition to make concessions. Their fatalism about left-wing politicians looks a bit too pessimistic from Europe, but it is also true that those historically successful left-wing politicians were only able to win their battles because of the disruptive power of those who pushed them upwards. They needed a twin-pronged strategy of infiltrating political institutions and the threat of societal disruption.

Unrest from the base has to be carefully constructed: one only has to watch the repression in the wake of some riots, cheered on by many ordinary people, to realise that if organisers can't sell to their peers a moral narrative behind their unrest, they leave their organisation open to the full force of the state being wielded against them. In the Glasgow rent strikes, the state undoubtedly felt limited in its actions by the strength of the narrative that the women were having to defend themselves while their menfolk were off defending the country. The disruption that tenant unions can bring to bear, including but not limited to widespread rent strike, must be legible to ordinary people as an understandable, even necessary action.

There is another element that must often be in place for people to accept that disruption has a worthwhile purpose: a positive vision must be offered that makes sense to people. My own research has shown that people want to understand how housing, through their action, will become better for them and those they love. And those who are watching the action must be able to understand it too, at least to some extent. A rent strike, no matter how generalised, will only ever involve a minority of the population in countries where home ownership is high. That makes it necessary in the UK and the US to persuade the homeowners – or at least some significant slice of them – that disruption is necessary so that they don't line up behind repression.

For most people, their definition of what makes a certain set of actions politically 'necessary' is not only that the status quo is bad, but that the action can be seen to lead towards an outcome that is visibly and understandably better. There needs to be a comprehensible path from here to there. Is the solution more public housing? That's a good start, but it may be necessary to address the fact that many people in public housing hate their landlords and want to escape into home ownership. If people in public housing can't get excited by a union's vision of more public housing, the organisation will have a problem persuading others. Is the solution more collectively owned housing co-operatives? That's half a vision, for then it is necessary to explain how a solution that has stayed so small in most countries can be scaled up. Is your strategy for better housing that we build autonomous community such that communities can self-provision? To get wide buy-in you might have to offer an economic model for how new housing gets built. Is the solution public–commons partnership where municipal governments partner with communities to create housing under democratic community control – the solution recently advocated by Keir Milburn, Bertie Russell and others?[6] That sounds exciting, but it will need to be proved possible by a viable economic settlement that redirects money from the private sector into commons projects. In search of practical visions, it will also be well worth tenant unions looking to the Global South, where large housing projects have often been initiated by large social movements, and significant resources diverted to long-term community-building. This touches upon a significant debate within parts of the left about whether grassroots activity is required to offer positive alternatives or whether it is sufficient to simply resist the status quo. It seems to me this debate is often too focused on whether the ruling class can understand an organisation or movement to have a positive vision or not, which is usually not the interesting question. Rather, the question is whether our peers – other people working and struggling like ourselves – can understand what end the organising is attempting to bring about. To Irish tenant union CATU, who publish their clear vision of housing on their website, it seems natural to offer this, but many tenant unions steer clear of getting more concrete in their housing vision for fear of the division it might cause. This is understandable when libertarian and orthodox socialists are in alliance, for their goals are sometimes genuinely rather different, yet the aversion to resolving the tensions could be seen as a contradictory position when tenant unions are explicitly aiming to build power. If power means anything, it means the ability to put a vision into practice. Any movement divided now, when it doesn't have power, will be divided when it does, and that will enable its enemies to tear it apart. And as mentioned, my own research suggests that those joining tenant unions who aren't animated by the downfall of capitalism – and in a successful union there should be many of them – are more likely to want a clear, achievable vision of the housing system. A project aiming to gain power must learn to develop some degree of unity and clarity of vision or risk seeming unserious about the possibility of winning.

Tenant unions face a future, then, where their ability to cause disruption is key. The disruption may be a generalised rent strike, but there are other options too. A tenant movement might aim to make the lives of property agents unbearable and the work of bailiffs impossible. Perhaps it might choose a token rent strike, such as everyone leaving 30 pence or 30 cents off their rent, signalling that tenants need rent to be no more than 30 per cent of their take-home pay, leaving landlords with the choice of ignoring the shortfall or clogging up the courts for petty amounts. Perhaps the disruption will be some form of unified tenant union and trade union action. The Glasgow rent strikes teach us that this disruption must not happen in isolation, it must be embedded in a society that is ready to organise alongside tenant unions and that understands the purpose of the particular action.

Tenant unions must build alliances as though their success depends on it, and many of them are already doing this. The national and international tenant union alliances forming are a good start, but more diverse partners must also be enlisted. Thinking through such alliances offers some potential positive directions to take. If new labour organising is happening primarily in insecure service jobs at Amazon or Starbucks or McDonald's, perhaps it makes sense that tenant unions should be directing their recruiting at those workplaces too, within the limit that they must organise those workers into geographically co-located organising units. This might bring housing organising and workplace organising into alignment with little effort, potentially strengthening both. In a rentier economy, those who own both the means of production and the assets we need to live must be constantly challenged, and a radical confrontation with the ruling class today might start not by seizing factories but by seizing homes.

VISIONS OF A WELL-HOUSED WORLD

Tenant union organisers are under no illusions about how difficult it will be to shift the status quo of 'housing crisis' in the current conjuncture. But across the Global North tenant unions are growing, and are committed to long-term organising that will shift the balance of power between tenants and landlords, even between tenants and the rentier class. They constitute a bold move to build new institutions of the left, and to embed a culture of organising among ordinary people. As tenant unions struggle for better housing, they also reconstitute community, challenging neoliberal culture as well as the rentierism that has flourished under the status quo. Tenant unions are a step towards a different economy and a different society, in which good housing is assured for everyone, by everyone. Some Latin American movements offer language that goes beyond this that clarifies the social embeddedness of housing solutions. They speak of the collective production of 'habitat', of which good housing is but a part, to emphasise that the task is to build a society focused on supporting each other.

What does victory look like? We know that it begins with significant numbers of tenants organised in tenant unions. For the remainder we must speculate a little. Perhaps the tenant union surge grows stronger as workplace unions grow stronger. Hand in hand the workplace and community organisers politicise an entire generation to understand that decent wages and decent housing are not only achievable, but make for a healthier and happier society. The common sense of what is achievable shifts, and governments once again understand that they need to solve 'the housing crisis', first, by not making it worse, and second, by treating housing as a right more important than the property and investment rights of a few.

Or perhaps the change will come through a more conflictual route. Perhaps zombie neoliberalism, animated by a new authoritarian tendency, will refuse to countenance any improvement in housing, pretending that the market will solve it despite decades of failure. Housing conditions get worse and housing more expensive. With hundreds of thousands of members behind them, tenant unions will decide they must bring the economy to a halt with a massive rent strike. Perhaps the strike is assisted by radical neighbourhood associations that resist every eviction. The banks to whom landlords owe money start to suffer as their previously steady income stream is interrupted. The government orders attacks on eviction resisters, but too many ordinary people are on their side. The police find they must crack the heads of mothers and grandfathers to get to the eviction resisters and even the centre-right press begin to find the level of violence distasteful. The government introduces rent controls but it is too little too late. The rent controls only keep the rents where they are, which is too high. Tenant movements demand a building programme of housing controlled by the community it sits within.

The government, eager not to create state-owned housing, takes the offer of developing public–commons partnerships with tenant unions and neighbourhood associations, providing resources to build or compulsorily purchase from landlords hundreds of thousands of properties that are controlled by communities. The government hesitates and prevaricates, and every time they do, tenant unions strike again. And gradually, the housing waiting lists that seemed unassailable melt away as properties are transferred into community hands. Bad landlords find they have no one to let their properties to and sell up. As rents fall, people have more money in their pockets and the malnutrition that dogs supposedly 'rich' economies melts away. Not only has housing become better, cheaper and more secure, but people are living better lives, wealthier in both money and community connections. People look back on the era of neoliberalism with disbelief. 'Imagine being stuck in that world where everyone in power pretended housing crisis couldn't be solved!' people will say to each other. 'What madness it was! What self-interested dishonesty!' And it all started, they will remember, when tenants got together and said that they weren't willing to accept it anymore.

To the renter now reading this in poor, expensive, insecure housing, these may seem like distant dreams. But part of the purpose of social movements is to allow people to dream and imagine again. Conversely, the purpose of repression, as academic and activist David Graeber liked to point out, was to prevent people dreaming. The dream becomes less distant the more people organise and resist repression. What was once only imagined becomes reality through the creation of a new power in the world, a power formed through the rewarding, everyday labour of building tenant unions. If you have not already started to organise as a tenant and with tenants, it is time to start now. Victory for tenant unions begins with us each making the choice to join the struggle.

Notes

CHAPTER 1

1. Potter, Allie. 2022. 'Tucson Tenants Protest Rent Hike at Monterey Garden Apartments'. www.kold.com (accessed 21 August 2023).
2. Tucson Tenants Union. 2022. 'Elder Displacement and Dispossession, Capital Accumulation in Tucson'. *Medium*. https://medium.com/@tucsontenantsunion/elder-displacement-and-dispossession-capital-accumulation-in-tucson-258d08bbb8ea (accessed 21 August 2023).
3. Office for National Statistics. 2021. *Housing, England and Wales: Census 2021*. www.ons.gov.uk/census/maps/choropleth/housing/tenure-of-household/hh-tenure-5a/owned-owns-outright (accessed 1 September 2024).
4. Balogun, B., Barton, C., Rankl, F., Bolton, P., Harker, R., & Wilson, W. 2024. *House of Commons Library Research Briefing: Health Inequalities: Cold or Damp Homes*. https://commonslibrary.parliament.uk/research-briefings/cbp-9696/.
5. Rolnik, R. (with Harvey, D. & Hirschhorn, F.). 2019. *Urban Warfare: Housing under the Empire of Finance*. London: Verso.
6. Harvey, David. 1978. 'The Urban Process under Capitalism: A Framework for Analysis'. *International Journal of Urban and Regional Research* 2(1–3): 101–31.
7. Piketty, Thomas. 2014. *Capital in the Twenty-First Century*. Cambridge, MA: The Belknap Press of Harvard University Press, p. 571.
8. Burn Murdoch, John. 2023. 'Home Ownership in Britain Has Become a Hereditary Privilege'. *Financial Times*. www.ft.com/content/985a608e-17a3-42ff-abb1-d78a10627a12 (accessed 20 July 2023).
9. Cork, Tristan. 2022. 'Excluded Campaigners Storm First Council Rent Commission Meeting'. *BristolLive*. www.bristolpost.co.uk/news/bristol-news/renters-storm-city-hall-stop-7384141 (accessed 22 September 2023).
10. Milburn, Keir. 2019. *Generation Left*. 1st edition. Cambridge and Medford, MA: Polity.
11. Since this is not a work of deep ethnography I should warn readers that none of the narratives of tenant unions in this book can be seen as

reflecting all possible narratives that exist in a union. Like all organising, tenant organising is often riven with disagreements – often productive, sometimes frustrating, occasionally toxic – about means and ends. It will take a more definitive history than this overview to outline all the streams of thought that have formed significant currents in today's tenant unions. I apologise in advance if anyone feels misrepresented.

12. 'Crown Heights Tenant Union: Building Power One Building at a Time'. https://indypendent.org/2016/04/crown-heights-tenant-union-building-power-one-building-at-a-time/ (accessed 9 August 2023).

13. Tenancy is not necessarily such an important category in poor countries, where 'peasant', 'worker', 'squatter', 'landless' or other identities are often more significant, including in housing organising.

CHAPTER 4

1. Porter, Catherine. 2020. Unpublished thesis: 'Exploring and Supporting Tenant Activism in Upstate New York'. Syracuse University.

2. Christophers, B. 2023. *Our Lives in Their Portfolios: Why Asset Managers Own the World*. London: Verso.

3. There has not been space in this book to delve far into the history of tenant organising and previous waves of tenant union organising. These range from early twentieth-century organising in much of Europe to a wave of US tenant unions emerging from the 1960s counterculture, such as San Francisco Tenant Union.

CHAPTER 5

1. As with much of the book, this applies mostly to the more autonomous tenant unions. There are many non-profit tenant organisations that see developers as their potential allies.

2. Vancouver Tenants Union. May 2022. *Basis of Unity Booklet*.

3. Robbins, Glyn. 2022. 'New York's Housing Justice Movement: Facing the COVID Eviction Cliff Edge'. *City* 26(4): 610–29.

4. Smucker, J.M. 2017. *Hegemony How-to: A Roadmap for Radicals*. Chico, CA: AK Press.

5. Bano, N. 2024. *Against Landlords: How to Solve the Housing Crisis*. London: Verso.

CHAPTER 6

1. York South-Weston Tenant Union. 6 October 2023. 'Largest Rent Strike in Toronto's History, as Two More Buildings Join'. www.tenantunion.ca/makinghistory (accessed 22 April 2024).
2. Englander, D. 1983. *Landlord and Tenant in Urban Britain, 1838–1918*. Oxford: Clarendon Press.
   Gray, N. (Ed.). 2018. *Rent and Its Dicontents: A Century of Housing Struggle*. London and New York: Rowman & Littlefield International.
3. Adkins, L., Cooper, M. & Konings, M. 2020. *The Asset Economy*. 1st edition. Medford, MA: Polity.
4. Englert, S. 2020. 'Notes on Organisation'. *Notes From Below*. https://notesfrombelow.org/article/notes-organisation.
5. Piven, F.F., & Cloward, R.A. 1979. *Poor People's Movements: Why They Succeed, How They Fail*. New York: Vintage Books.
6. Common Wealth. 2019. *Public-Common Partnerships: Building New Circuits of Collective Ownership Report*. www.common-wealth.org/publications/public-common-partnerships-building-new-circuits-of-collective-ownership (accessed 19 September 2024).

Index

The Pluto Press Newsletter

Hello friend of Pluto!

Want to stay on top of the best radical books
we publish?

Then sign up to be the first to hear about our
new books, as well as special events,
podcasts and videos.

You'll also get 50% off your first order with us
when you sign up.

Come and join us!

Go to bit.ly/PlutoNewsletter

Thanks to our Patreon subscriber:

Ciaran Kane

Who has shown generosity and comradeship in support of our publishing.

Check out the other perks you get by subscribing to our Patreon – visit patreon.com/plutopress.

Subscriptions start from £3 a month.